A Visit from Father

A · WARDLAW · BOOK

A Visit from Father

AND OTHER TALES OF THE MOJAVE

Don Worcester

Texas A&M University Press
COLLEGE STATION

"A Visit from Father" was published in *The Roundup,* journal of Western Writers of America, in 1970. "Coyote" appeared in *Far West* in 1980.

Frontispiece: Sketch for "A Little Shade," by Tom Lea

The paper used in this book meets the minimum requirements of the American National Standard for Permanence of Paper for Printed Library Materials, Z39.48-1984. Binding materials have been chosen for durability.
∞

Library of Congress Cataloging-in-Publication Data

Worcester, Donald Emmet, 1915–
    A visit from father and other tales of the Mojave / Don Worcester. — 1st ed.
        p. cm. — (A Wardlaw book)
        ISBN 0-89096-429-7 (alk. paper)
        1. Mojave Desert (Calif.)—Social life and customs. 2. Mojave Desert (Calif.)—Description and travel. 3. Worcester, Donald Emmet, 1915– —Childhood and youth. I. Title. II. Series.
F868.M65W67 1990
979.4'95—dc20   89-5103
                                                          CIP

To the memory of my brother Harris

Contents

A Word of Acknowledgment   xi
Publisher's Acknowledgment   xiii
Arizona   3
The Itinerary   4
Early Memories   6
Parents and Grandparents   13
The Old Homestead   18
Rattlesnakes   24
Long Ears and Short   26
School Bus Days   29
Runaways   33
A Walk in the Snow   35
World's Champion Coyote
  Yipper   37
Round Mountain   39
First Levis   41
Riley   42
Wolf   44
Berkeley   46

Ace   47
Rex   49
A Visit from Father   52
The Hammerhead Kicker   56
Desert Ride   57
Goodbye to the
  Homestead   60
Winter Park   62
Arizona Again   65
Bull Riding   67
Apache Land   69
Kinishba   71
Last Visit   74
Bard College   75
Attachment to Horses   80
Graduate School   81
Harris   86
Palmdale   88
Coyote   92

Illustrations

"A Little Shade," by Tom Lea	*Frontispiece*
Father with Lavon and Don	*Page* 6
Don	7
Harris	8
Lavon and Don	9
Mother before flight to Tucson, 1919	10
Curtis Hispano plane, 1919	11
Grandfather Makemson, Father, Mable, and Harvey	12
Grandfather Worcester as a young man	14
Lavon, Mother, and Don, near Riverside	17
Dr. Maud W. Makemson, Vassar College Observatory	18
Harris, Lavon, Alan, and Kirke in 1914 Ford	20
Kirke, grandmother, grandfather, Lavon, Alan, Don, and Richard	22
Harris, Lavon, Mother, and Don, 1935	64
Don and Apache friend, David Kane, 1936	70
Don and Dean Byron Cummings, Kinishba, 1941	72
Don	77
Dr. Maud W. Makemson at telescope	83
Barbara and Don	85
Don and Harris	87
Harris	89

A Word of Acknowledgment

I wrote "A Visit from Father" in 1949 or 1950, not long after receiving a letter from a lawyer in Phoenix informing me that my father's will was in probate. About twenty years later I discovered it in my files and sent it to *The Roundup*. When it appeared in July 1970, Jeanne Williams urged me to write a book of recollections about growing up under conditions unfamiliar to most people today, and my family concurred. I tried to comply, but reliving some of those years I found painful and depressing, which is why it took so long to write so little. When colleague Jim Corder's *Lost in West Texas* appeared in this same series, I showed him my manuscript, which had been untouched for several years. He made helpful suggestions and recommended sending it to Lloyd Lyman, at that time director of Texas A&M University Press. I thank all of the above for their encouragement and patience.

Publisher's Acknowledgment

The Texas A&M University Press is privileged to add its imprint to this Wardlaw Book. The designation claims a special place in the list of Texas A&M publications.

Supported with funds inspired by the initiative of Chester Kerr, former head of Yale University Press, this book, along with its companion volumes, perpetuates the association of Frank H. Wardlaw's name with a select group of titles appropriate to his reputation as man of letters, distinguished publisher, and founder of three university presses.

Donors of these funds represent a wide cross-section of Frank Wardlaw's admirers, including colleagues from scholarly presses throughout the country as well as those from other callings who recognize and applaud the many contributions that he has made to scholarship, literature, and publishing in his four decades of active service.

The Texas A&M University Press acknowledges with profound appreciation these donors.

Mr. Herbert S. Bailey, Jr.
Mr. Robert Barnes
Mr. W. Walker Cowen
Mr. Robert S. Davis
Mr. John Ervin, Jr.
Mr. William D. Fitch
Mr. August Frugé
Mr. David H. Gilbert
Mr. Kenneth Johnson
Mr. Chester Kerr
Mr. Robert T. King
Mr. Carl C. Krueger, Jr.

Mr. John H. Kyle
John and Sara Lindsey
Mrs. S. M. McAshan, Jr.
Mr. Kenneth E. Montague
Mr. Edward J. Mosher
Mrs. Florence Rosengren
Mr. Jack Schulman
Mr. C. B. Smith
Mr. Richard A. Smith
Mr. Stanley Sommers
Dr. Frank E. Vandiver
Ms. Maud E. Wilcox

Mr. John Williams

Their bounty has assured that Wardlaw Books will be a special source of instruction and entertainment to the reading public for many years to come.

A Visit from Father

Arizona

As far back as I can remember, for my brother Harris and me Arizona was a magical name, our dreamland. Even before we started school we talked often of going back. I have never gotten over that desire to return there to live. I'm not entirely sure what inspired this feeling, but even today if I see Arizona mentioned in article or book, I must read it. In a sense, I guess, it's the nostalgia of the expatriate.

It couldn't have been because of a thorough acquaintance with the state, for I was only four or five when we left, and I didn't see it even briefly for twelve years, but that made no difference. Arizona was, I knew, a land of cowboys and Indians, and both ranked high in my esteem. It was also where our father lived, and even though our mother had divorced him after he wandered off and didn't return, we knew he was somewhere in Arizona and always hoped he'd come and take us there. Our mother was away teaching school or going to the University of California in Berkeley, and living with grandparents wasn't the same as living with father or mother, even though they did what they considered right and proper for us. They hoped Harris and I might amount to something some day, but had serious and often-expressed doubts about me. I'm sure that must have heightened my feeling for Arizona.

I must have been responsible for infecting Harris with the longing for Arizona, for he was only about two when we left. Whatever the reason, we literally ached to return to what we proudly considered our native state and real home. I even envied Harris for having been born in Cochise County—that sounded better than Maricopa County, where I was born, for Cochise had been a famous Apache chief.

The Itinerary

The homestead was between Little Rock and Big Rock creeks, but closer to the latter. When we climbed high enough in the mountains behind the homestead, we could see two grayish streaks of boulders marking the courses of the two creeks clear across the desert to Muroc Dry Lake. Muroc was a tiny settlement near the huge lake bed. I rode the school bus there once and spent a night with a friend. As we neared the lake bed it appeared blue, and one could see the reflection of trees in it, as if it were full of water. Newcomers were always told that there had been a big rain and the lake was full, but it was an optical illusion. Today the lake bed is a landing field for spacecraft.

My growing up years involved living temporarily in a number of places, and my recollections of some of them are hazy. Arizona was for years more of a symbol than the scene of pleasant experiences that stand out sharply in my memory. We were living in the little copper mining town of Bisbee when Harris was born, but I was only two at the time. Later we lived in Phoenix for several years before going to Pasadena, which I remember only as the place we started from on the first junket to the homestead.

The Mojave Desert, which eons ago must have been a well-watered garden spot judging by all the dry creek beds, was a vast, arid expanse with distant buttes, a few small towns, and occasional prospectors with pack burros, still hoping to strike it rich. Little Rock, which had ample water from the dam in Little Rock Creek, was a pear growing center with a general store, a blacksmith shop that was soon converted into a garage, a gas pump, an elementary school, and a county library in some family's living room.

Palmdale was a little town in which most families, Mexican and Anglo, worked for the railroad, although there were farms and dairies around it. Lancaster was much larger and more prosperous because of the high quality alfalfa hay produced there. It had a high school to which students were bussed daily as much as fifty miles each way and from all directions. For those living farther away, there were dormitories.

Round Mountain, in northern California's Shasta County, was an isolated hamlet with one store and a dozen houses. The school we went to was not the one in town but a little one-room affair located among towering pines and within walking distance of half a dozen or more farm families. Most of the country was open cattle range and forest. We had a daily view of both Mount Shasta and the volcano Mount Lassen.

Berkeley was in those days a pleasant university town from which many people commuted daily by ferryboat to San Francisco. Commuters would throw pieces of bread to the seagulls circling around them, and we loved riding on the ferryboats. I believe I read that after the Bay Bridge was built the ferries were all sold to Brazil. Berkeley was the first real city we lived in after leaving Phoenix, and where I became acquainted with city life.

Winter Park, Florida, had quite a few northern families who had winter homes there before the depression struck while they were there and they were obliged to remain. In other ways it was probably a typical Southern college town, although Rollins, with many northern and foreign students, was not a typical Southern college.

Poughkeepsie, New York, was an industrial city on the Hudson, with Vassar College on its periphery. In the surrounding area were many prosperous farms and attractive little towns like Millbrook, Hyde Park, where Franklin D. Roosevelt's estate was, and Rhinebeck, which boasted an eighteenth century inn still in operation. Poughkeepsie is where we first learned about long, cold, and sunless winters. Once while we were there the Hudson froze solidly enough for people to drive across it in cars.

Tucson was another university city and winter resort, with a mixed population. Its roots go back to the seventeenth or early eighteenth century, when the mission of San Xavier del Bac was founded and a Spanish *presidio* was located nearby.

Gainesville, Florida, was a little university town of about 20,000 when we moved there in 1947, but over the years both town and university have increased enormously. Except for a semester in Ann Arbor, Michigan, and a year at the University of Madrid, these were the places where I lived at least briefly before moving to Fort Worth in 1963 and to our ranchito in Parker County four years later.

Father with Lavon and baby Don

Early Memories

One of my few vivid memories of my father was at the Arizona State Fair in Phoenix, probably in 1918, when I was a white-haired three-year-old. He wore jeans, boots, and a straw sombrero. Lean, wiry, with brown hair and eyes, he looked like a typical rancher or cowboy. One of the agricultural exhibits at the fair was a spike-wheeled tractor that had the steering wheel tied so that it roared around in a small, tight circle, churning up the ground. My father walked toward it.

"Emmet, where are you going?" my mother asked.

"Just lookin'," he replied. "Sure could use one of these."

When the tractor roared by him again he hopped onto it and sat happily behind the steering wheel while it continued its endless

6

Don

circling. I felt proud of him but afraid he'd get run over by those mean-looking wheels.

My mother snorted. "Let's go before he gets himself killed," she said. Carrying Harris, who was only a year old, she led Lavon and me to another exhibit. I kept looking back and stumbling along until my father hopped nimbly down and hurried after us.

Another memory of the fair was a stunt man crawling around on the wings of a slow-moving biplane flying back and forth in front of the grandstand. I held my breath while he hung by his knees from the landing gear, then climbed up and stood on his head in front of the wings just behind the whirling propeller. At least that's the

Harris

way I remember it. There was also a hot air balloon that lifted off and floated right over us.

One morning I saw blue raccoon tracks all over the walls on the porch of the little house where we lived. Our pet raccoon had opened a bottle of bluing, dipped his paws in it, and then decorated the walls. Bluing was something used in washing clothes in those days. I don't know what it did for dirty clothes, but it made attractive decorations when properly applied.

That house had other and less pleasant memories for me. In the center was a small, square hall, with four doors opening into it. One morning my grandmother, who was staying with us while my mother was at work on a newspaper, discovered a large, wet spot in my bed. She had a razor strap in one hand and grasped my arm in the other, dragging me into the hall. When she closed the doors so the neighbors couldn't hear me squall, the place was dark and terrifying.

Lavon and Don

"If you're too lazy to get out of bed when you have to go," she said, "this is what you deserve," and she let me have it.

She was a determined enemy of sloth and laziness, and always met them head on. Since one character-building treatment failed to cure me of those sins, she regarded me as incorrigible, but that didn't discourage her. I was a challenge, and she persevered with a will that I might have considered admirable under other circumstances. She didn't know it, but I would gladly have abandoned even more attractive habits just to escape those early morning character conditioners. I could never convince her that it wasn't a conscious, malicious act.

There were three of us children—Lavon, who was two years older than I, was blond and near-sighted, and had to wear glasses when she started school. Harris, who was two years younger than I, had brown hair and brown eyes and was small-boned and slender like

9

Mother before flight to Tucson, 1919

our father. Lavon was born in Pasadena before the family moved to Arizona. I was born in an adobe ranch house near Tempe in 1915, and Harris was born in Bisbee, where my father worked briefly in one of the copper mines. We must have lived there a year or two, for that's where we were I think, when my father got the wanderlust and left.

My mother got a job as a proofreader or copy editor on the Bisbee paper. She had attended Girls Latin School in Boston and Radcliffe College for a year before the family moved to California, and she easily convinced the people on the paper that she was more literate than any of them. Before long she was a reporter, and soon was hired by the *Arizona Gazette* in Phoenix. In June 1919, when the first mail plane, a World War I vintage Curtis Hispano biplane, made the flight from Phoenix to Tucson, she was the reporter chosen to make the trip and write a report on it. One of the reporters was so outraged to see a woman receive this rare honor that he quit.

Curtis Hispano plane ready for first air mail run from Phoenix to Tucson, 1919

Our paternal grandparents had a dairy farm near Glendale, not far from Phoenix, and we lived with them for a few months. That's where we were when I scored a small triumph by tying my shoelaces for the first time. I was so proud of the feat that I ran to tell someone about it, forgetting that I had on another shoe, so I tripped over the laces and fell ankles over teakettle. One morning I ran all over the farm with a salt shaker in my hand. My grandfather had placed his hand on my shock of white hair and handed me the shaker. "If you sprinkle salt on a bird's tail," he told me with a twinkle in his eyes, "you can catch it." Maybe so. I tried for several hours but never got close enough to a bird to test it. This grandfather took me wherever he went and was friendly and talkative. I would gladly have stayed there.

Because my hair was white they naturally called me "cottontop," a name I despised. I remember wishing I'd been born an Indian so that I'd have black hair. One's perspective on these minor matters changes over the years, I learned. My hair is white again, what there is left of it, but now I'm more interested in quantity than color.

Another memory of Phoenix was of a huge tank wagon drawn by a team of large horses to sprinkle down the dust on the unpaved street past the little house where we lived. We neighborhood urchins all ran barefooted after the wagon to get sprinkled along with the dust. And on higher ground not far away was a big corral full

Grandfather Makemson, Father, Mable, and Harvey

of horses and mules, which required frequent inspections by me.

One other memory of those days was of people running around shouting and acting happy. I learned later that that was the day Phoenix folks learned that the armistice had been signed and World War I was over.

The next year our aunt Mable, my father's sister, took the three of us to Pasadena on the train. Late in the afternoon it stopped and men got out and walked ahead. We looked out to see what was going on. Ahead of us a river was flowing over its banks; the railroad tracks disappeared at the water's edge. The train backed up to some railroad station where we spent a miserable night trying to sleep on benches in a crowded and sweltering waiting room.

When we finally got to Pasadena my mother, her sister Isabelle, and our maternal grandparents were sitting in the living room looking solemn. Years later I learned that my mother's only brother, Ira, had just died in the postwar influenza epidemic.

I was too young to know much about what was going on at that time, but my mother was still working on the Phoenix newspaper. I was much attached to her—we all were—and life wasn't the same without her. But she had to support herself and us, which wasn't easy for a woman in those days.

I still remember wondering when we'd see her again. She came from Arizona for a visit one time, taking the train to Victorville. I got to accompany my grandfather when he went to meet her, and we headed across the desert on dirt roads. We got lost a few times and stuck in the sand once, for those hard little high pressure tires on his Model T truck didn't have much traction. He let some of the air out of the rear tires, enough to get the truck out of the sand, then had to pump them up again. At any rate we managed to meet the train on time. I forget how long my mother stayed, but it seemed pretty short to us kids. I don't know where she went next, but her departure left us feeling forlorn.

Parents and Grandparents

My California grandfather—Gene, my grandmother called him—was a wiry man about five feet, ten inches tall, blue-eyed, with a slightly jutting jaw, neatly trimmed gray mustache, and a New England accent. He'd been raised on a farm in Vermont, and although he was a skillful cabinetmaker and carpenter by trade, he was always a farmer at heart. He was a strong union man and by political persuasion a Socialist. He should have stayed in some town or city where he could have earned a decent living, but he was powerfully drawn to the land. He chose a bad time to take up farming in southern California. He was gruff and said little to anyone, so we were in awe of him most of the time. He thought kids should make themselves useful, so we were often obliged to pull weeds all day in his cornfields.

He had gone to sea for a short time as a boy, and I guess that's where he learned profanity and his ideas concerning punishment. He goddamned everything, and one of his favorite rejoinders was

Grandfather Worcester as a young man

"touch hole!" My grandmother explained that he was referring to the place a lighted match was used to set off the gunpowder in old-time cannons. We lost a little respect for him over that, but he made up for it with other expressions. When he was deeply moved his swearing was descriptive, eloquent, and a joy to hear unless one was the cause of it. His notions of punishment were either laying on with a stout willow rod or, if he was enraged, a kick in the crotch. I got that treatment only once, but it made a lasting impression. My grandmother was screaming and trying to stop him, unfortunately without success.

My grandmother, whose name was Fanny, was from Ohio and she was proud of the fact that she was a direct descendant of Peregrine White, who was born on the *Mayflower* or soon after it landed, if I remember correctly. I never knew how much education either of them had, but both used the English language correctly and insisted that we do the same, for which I am grateful. She didn't allow us to use any of the common racist epithets for minority groups, so we grew up without such terms becoming part of our vocabulary. For this, too, I am grateful.

It was a hard life for her, and I know she deserved better. She was always hoping they could sell the homestead and move to town, but it never happened. She was always delighted and extremely hospitable on the rare occasions we had visitors, for hers was a lonely life. She had no use for our father, which I suppose was natural since he remarried after the divorce, and we quickly learned not to mention him in her presence. When she was miffed at me she called me Emmet, my father's name and my middle one. I was supposed to be crushed by that—but, perverse wretch that I was, I secretly enjoyed it. I was careful to conceal the fact, for revealing it would have made me, in her eyes, "an ungrateful brat." We three kids talked about our father when we were alone and dreamed of him coming to visit us.

I always felt that my grandmother ranked me last or actually disliked me, but our friend A. P. Aldrich assured me that wasn't true. It was simply that Harris was much more affectionate than I, and there's no doubt that she needed affection. She could always pry secrets out of him, which got me into trouble more than once. She played one trick on us that left open wounds for a while. Our aunt Mable wrote from Phoenix and sent presents occasionally, always including all three of us. Once a Brownie camera arrived from her, and my grandmother said it was a present for Lavon—there was nothing for Harris and me. We were both crushed, and couldn't understand why we had been left out. Years later we learned that the camera was a gift to the three of us, but my grandmother, knowing that Harris and I probably would wreck it the moment we got our hands on it, decided to exclude us.

One time my grandmother planned a birthday party for me, and sent invitations to the mothers of four or five boys my age who lived reasonably near. She baked a cake, made lemonade, and in general went to the trouble of making the party a success. We were all excited about it, especially me, for I'd never had a birthday party before. Harris and I walked down the road a little way to greet people as they arrived. The morning passed, and nobody came. After while we speculated some as to why they were all late. Finally we realized that no one was coming. Not one of them ever mentioned it to me.

My mother, who was blond, blue-eyed, and attractive, found herself with the three of us to support. She was determined to make her way in pursuits usually dominated by men, such as reporting and astronomy. She was fond of her parents, and helped them whenever she could, but she wasn't pleased that they had named her Maud. There was a cartoon of a fractious mule: "And Her Name Was Maud," and I guess she took a lot of ribbing about that. She preferred to be called Nancy. Intelligent and well-read though she was, she was also an incurable romantic, and in our long walks together in the Berkeley hills I'm sure I caught the same bug. I guess one might call it a penchant for daydreaming. In Arizona, she said, she "commenced a career of raising cows, chickens, and children." On a picnic north of Phoenix in May 1921 she saw an extraordinary display of northern lights that occurred at the same time unusually large sunspots were observed. This aroused her interest in celestial matters, and she began reading books on astronomy. The more she read, the greater her interest grew.

After teaching school in Riverside for a year, she took the train to Berkeley to enter the University of California as a sophomore astronomy major. She arrived there a week or more early, for she needed to find a part-time job. But not getting busy with classes immediately gave her too much time to think. She became so homesick that she took the train back to Palmdale. I believe that was the year she taught there, and we were with her. She bought a Buick touring car, and on weekends we'd head for the homestead.

The next year, 1923, she left for Berkeley determined to stay, and although we watched for her to return, she remained. Somehow she managed to support herself and earn Phi Beta Kappa honors at the same time. Lavon was with her part of the time, but I think that was after she entered graduate school and earned a little more money.

Although I was too rattle-brained to appreciate it in those days, what she accomplished was rather remarkable. There were few women astronomers; it required extra ability and determination for her to succeed.

Although she got off to a late start—she was thirty-nine when she received a doctorate in astronomy—my mother still carved out

Lavon, Mother, and Don, near Riverside

a rather distinguished career. I don't know much about her astronomical research, but she received a Vassar College grant to study Polynesian astronomy and navigation at the Bishop Museum in Honolulu. Later she went on a Guggenheim Fellowship to study Mayan astronomy and calendar in the Yucatan and Guatemala.

After retiring as departmental chairman at Vassar in 1957, she taught astronomy and astrodynamics for several years at UCLA. While there she was co-author of *Introduction to Astrodynamics,* first published in 1960. In 1963, while still at UCLA, she was elected a Fellow of the American Association for the Advancement of Science.

Following her second retirement, she began a new career in space research at the Applied Research Laboratories of General Dynamics in Fort Worth. The result was undoubtedly her most significant research, which was a method of enabling astronauts to determine their positions on the far side of the moon, where they were unable to use radio or radar. Her method was described in an article titled "Determination of Seleonographic Positions," published in *The Moon,* an international journal, in 1971.

17

Dr. Maud W. Makemson with bust of astronomer Maria Mitchell, Vassar College Observatory

Mentally and physically active as long as her health and failing
eyesight enabled her to work, she then embarked on her last project,
translating from the Latin *The Astronomical System of Philolaus* by
Ismael Bullialdus, published in Paris in 1645. She died in Weather-
ford, Texas, in 1977 at the age of eighty-six.

The Old Homestead

About the time we got to Pasadena, our grandfather had traded his
house there for a homestead in the foothills on the edge of Antelope Valley and near the Mojave Desert. The first trip he and my
grandmother made to the homestead was in a one-horse wagon, and

it took them nearly a week. He chose a bad time and place to take up farming, for a drouth soon settled on the land, and he spent the rest of his life in a constant and losing struggle against poverty.

At the time, however, Antelope Valley seemed well watered and inviting country, with plenty of grass for cattle and spectacular wild-flowers. The snow was heavy on the San Gabriel Mountains, which lay between the Mojave and Los Angeles, and the creeks in the area flowed the year round. It remained that way for several years, then entered a cycle of increasing aridity.

In the same area were other homesteads owned by small ranchers whose cattle and horses ranged freely. The first year my grandfather bought a young half-wild bay mare he called Mountain Maid. He'd probably worked oxen when he was a boy, but he knew nothing about handling untrained range horses, and she broke away from him and went back to the range. We figured that she must have had a colt every year, and that after a while he owned a bunch of horses. I guess he knew he couldn't handle her or others like her, for he never asked any of the cowboys to catch her for him. We kids hoped for years that somehow we'd gather in his range stock, for horses were about all we were interested in.

Over the next few years the snow on the mountains gradually receded, and creeks like the one that ran through the homestead no longer had water in them the year round. There was no way to irrigate the alfalfa, and the field turned to foxtails and weeds. As the drouth continued, crops no longer grew; only the orchard, a strawberry patch, and a truck garden that could be watered from the spring survived. No one had any idea how long the drouth would continue, but my grandfather never gave up hope that it would end. He had to take jobs as a carpenter when they were available in order to pay his bill at the grocery store. He also raised sweet corn and string beans to sell at the store in Little Rock. He talked frequently of getting a well drilled so that he could irrigate more land, but he never had the money for it.

When my grandparents moved to the homestead in 1919 or 1920, we three children went with them, while my mother returned to Arizona to continue working on the *Arizona Gazette.* My grandfather had bought a 1914 Ford truck, a forerunner of the modern

Harris, Lavon, Alan (cousin), and Kirke (cousin) in the 1914 Ford

pickup. It was loaded high with family belongings; Lavon and I rode on top of the pile, for there wasn't any room for us inside. We were both scared going through the old Newhall tunnel. At the Oaks, a picnic ground in a live oak grove, we sat in the shade and ate sandwiches while the Ford's radiator cooled. The journey that now takes less than two hours took the entire day, part of it on gravel roads. Those old "tin lizzies" were sturdy vehicles for their day, but the engines frequently overheated and had to be cooled. They were also temperamental, and required frequent tinkering to get them cranked up and going again. The small tires carried sixty pounds of air pressure, and when one blew out it was like a blast from a large bore shotgun.

There were three pedals in the center. The left one was low gear, the middle one was reverse, and the one on the right was the brake. On the left of the driver was a long lever. When it was pulled back it was a brake for parking. Straight up was neutral; pushed forward was high gear—there was nothing between low and high.

Under the steering wheel were two levers. The one on the right was the accelerator; the one on the left was called the spark, for it controlled the amount of electricity from the dry cell battery to the spark plugs. There was no self-starter. To start the motor, you pushed the spark lever up to reduce the charge, then turned the motor over with a hand crank until it began firing or you became exhausted. If you forgot to lower the spark, the motor would kick backwards and throw you over the hood or maybe break your arm. Starting it was always an adventure.

The truck had no door on the driver's side, which caused some problems. When my grandfather stopped it, and sat there a moment or two with the motor idling, anyone sitting by the passenger door was in a quandary, not knowing whether or not to open the door and get out. Finally he'd shut the motor off and say, "*Well, get out!*" which caused a mad scramble. He drove the old truck for years, until it threw a piston rod through the block and had to be retired to the scrap heap.

The last part of that first trip before reaching the foothills was on a rutted road that went through a narrow passage called "The Cut." The banks on either side were higher than the truck. We got stuck in it late in the afternoon, and were terrified at the thought of having to spend the night there. But a man named George Pallett who lived about a mile away brought his team down and pulled us out.

The cabin on the homestead had a couple of small rooms and an attached shed where Harris and I slept for many years. A miserable little wood stove stood in one corner of the kitchen, which had a sink with running water from the spring, a sink shelf, and a table where we ate. One of my grandmother's many unfulfilled dreams was having one of the large ranges like those we saw in other people's kitchens. The elevation was about forty-five hundred feet above sea level and the ground froze solid at times in the winter. The little stove provided the only heat—heat was confined to the kitchen. When we had freezing weather, Harris and I heated rocks, wrapped them in old newspapers or whatever was available, stuck them in the bed, and used them for footwarmers. The shed where we slept was about the same temperature as it was outside.

On small farms in those days everything was done by hand or with

Back: Kirke, Grandmother, Grandfather, Lavon, and Alan; *front:* Don and Richard

animal power, for few labor-saving machines were affordable. One man or family could farm only a limited area, which explains why most homesteads on public land were only 160 acres. Such family farms usually raised most of the food the family needed, feed for the animals, and some crop that brought cash each year. In fertile regions with ample rainfall a family could manage fairly well on a homestead; elsewhere it was a life of extreme poverty. At least we didn't have doctor's bills in those days; the nearest doctor was in Lancaster, about forty miles away, so no one went to a doctor except for broken bones.

I remember watching my grandfather cut wheat with a scythe, so that it fell in neat rows. Using a rake with long wooden teeth, he formed little piles, tied a cord around each shock, then loaded them in the truck and hauled them up to the house. He stretched out a tarpaulin flat on the ground and piled the wheat on it. With a flail made of two pieces of scrub oak limbs, he thrashed it until the kernels were free. He and my grandmother each held corners of the tarp and threw the wheat into the air until the wind had blown the chaff away.

A creek fed by snow in the mountains a few miles above the place flowed the year round when we first arrived. Alongside it was the alfalfa field, irrigated by a ditch from the creek. Near the cabin was an apple orchard and some peach and plum trees. Every year but one a late frost killed most of the fruit. That one year my grandfather sold his apples for five hundred dollars. Other years we picked what apples there were and stored them in the cellar, to eat during the winter.

On the homestead our regular diet was built around Boston baked beans, which we ate almost every day, beans cooked in molasses with a bit of salt pork thrown in. Every Saturday or Sunday a week's supply was cooked, a process that took all day. In summer we had corn, string beans, and strawberries, and some fruits and vegetables were canned for winter. In addition to his truck garden my grandfather raised his own tobacco and grew hops for making home brew. His breakfast was exactly the same every morning—fried eggs, bacon, and fried potatoes. We kids ate oatmeal mush every morning, and most of the year had fresh milk. I have never once eaten oatmeal mush since leaving the homestead.

Since there wasn't an icehouse within miles, refrigeration was a problem. My grandfather built a cooler, a boxlike structure with shelves and the outside covered with burlap. On top was a big pan of water, which was allowed to dribble out and down all four sides to keep the burlap wet. Evaporation kept it reasonably cool inside, but nothing could be kept for long. The cooler sat in the shade of a scrub oak, its legs standing in cans of water to keep ants from invading. Hanging nearby was an *olla* similarly covered with burlap and kept wet so that the drinking water stayed cool. A long handled dipper hung near it.

When I was seven my mother bought me a little single-shot Stevens .22 rifle, and I shot cottontails, jackrabbits, and a few quail with it. It had a lever for extracting shells. Once when I was climbing over sandrocks with it in hand I slipped and fell. Somehow that lever clamped on the nail of my little finger and tore it out. I made the rocks echo, but it soon healed and another nail grew in.

When I was older I used my grandfather's 20-gauge shotgun. Occasionally someone loaned me a Winchester .30-30 rifle and a few shells, and I killed deer. I hunted only out of season, for it was too dangerous to hunt when there was a flock of strangers out hunting with high-powered rifles. They were likely to shoot at anything that moved. Game wardens didn't bother ranch people who killed deer to eat.

Hunting was only for food, not for pleasure, and I never considered it a sport. After leaving the homestead I hunted no more. When I first received the .22 I was so eager to kill something that I shot one of the towhees that were always around our woodpile. They were friendly, harmless little birds, and I still feel remorse whenever I think of it.

Rattlesnakes

We got acquainted with rattlesnakes almost immediately after we went to live on the homestead, for there were lots of diamondbacks around. My grandfather kept a dog chained at his alfalfa field along the creek to cut down on competition from jackrabbits and cottontails. We toddled down to visit the dog, which was usually glad for any company. It was standing at the end of its chain, growling and snarling. Coiled between it and the post it was chained to was a rattlesnake, with darting tongue and whirring rattles. I suppose we'd been warned about rattlesnakes, for we knew at once what it was and ran back up the hill screeching for our grandfather. He grabbed a hoe or shovel and dispatched it.

Once in the next year or two Harris and I were up on the lower part of the mountains two or three miles from the homestead. As we trotted down a deer trail I was in the air and coming down just as a rattler sidled across the trail. I tried desperately to defy the laws of gravity but failed and came down on it right behind its head. It was probably just a small mountain diamondback but it looked huge to me. My recollection is that I didn't touch the ground for at least fifty feet. I didn't know about adrenalin, but it must have been squirting, and I was squalling at the top of my voice. From that scary experience I figured out how birds were invented—some creature stepped on a rattlesnake and jumped so high he grew feathers before he came back to earth.

Later, but still before we'd started school, Harris and I were wandering around, as we did every day. We climbed on a big rock and were ready to jump onto a yerba scenta bush at the base of it when I saw a rattler coiled up asleep in its shade. We made such a racket that the snake woke up, gave us a warning whir with its rattles, and slithered down a squirrel hole. We piled rocks over the hole and left, returning in a few days with long poles. We removed the rocks and the snake came right out and started crawling away. We hopped around it and pounded it to death. No dragon slayers were prouder of their first dragon than we were of our first rattler.

We killed many of them after that—they're easily killed if one simply stays out of range. Many years later I saw a rattler going along minding its own business and let it go unmolested. I mentioned it to our neighbor A. P. Aldrich, who was the nearest thing to a father that Harris and I had.

"What if it bit a friend of yours?" he asked. I didn't have any friends to speak of, but it was a good question. I still don't like killing rattlesnakes and leave them alone unless they're near the house or where we have small colts.

We always went barefooted, by choice as well as necessity, even to school. Because of the snakes we learned to be extremely careful where we put our feet down. But late one afternoon Harris had gone down to the pasture to drive the cow up for milking when I heard him screeching. He was barefooted, and he'd been looking for the cow instead of where he put his feet and had stepped right on a rattler that was coiled up asleep. Harris was talking pretty fast and trying to walk without touching the ground. I gathered from a few things he said that the feel of a bare foot on a coiled snake was unsettling. I agreed, for I remembered that stepping on one not even coiled had made an impression on me.

We had a dog of undetermined ancestry named Sally who got bitten on the nose by a rattler. We were all making a fuss over her, afraid the bite might be fatal. She enjoyed the attention and sympathy, suffering majestically for our benefit. When my grandfather came along and saw her swollen nose he started laughing. She wagged her tail and quit putting us on.

Long Ears and Short

After we'd been on the homestead a year or two an old burro wandered in and stayed with us a while. He was gentle, slow-moving, and not highly motivated, which made him just right for us. We rode him off on roads and trails; he gave us our start at riding.

Once right after the Fourth of July, I was sitting on him and feeling like a five- or six-year-old cowboy when Harris came running up and stuck a cap pistol under the burro's nose.

"Don't shoot!" I screeched at him.

"Why?" he asked and pulled the trigger. I was about to explain that it would scare the burro when I found myself flat on the ground with a mouthful of dirt.

Another burro joined us later, and we rode him when he was in the mood for it. When he wasn't he put his head between his front legs, humped his back, and hopped a couple of times; the rider always slid off over his neck. We called him Dynamite, but he wasn't taken in by flattery. I came upon him once after I'd walked about eight miles and figured I'd ride him the last three miles home. He liked it where he was, and after he'd thrown me twice I went on my way on foot.

Riding burros was just a step toward riding horses, for that was our real goal. Even when we were making do with burros, from the time we were old enough to think about it, Harris and I tried to catch range horses, figuring if we had something respectable to ride we could make it to Arizona for sure. We'd wrap short ropes around our waists, stick an apple in a pocket of our bib overalls, and head off across the foothills. The horses were the ones that the ranchers had left behind when they moved out. They weren't wild, as their offspring would be in a few years, but they weren't willing to be caught by a couple of long-haired, barefoot, homestead kids. That was just as well, for we hadn't ever figured out what we'd do with one if we caught it. We kept trying year after year, nevertheless, from the time I was about seven.

One time we'd crossed over the foothills to where the old Matthews ranch had been. The house had burned down about the time they sold off their cattle, and they had moved away, leaving their horses behind. We found five or six horses in a box canyon, a canyon with only one exit or entrance. We walked toward them like a couple of happy idiots, making cooing sounds and holding out applecores for them to eat. We'd gotten hungry on the long hike getting there, and that's all we'd saved for them. The horses apparently were offended at the sight of apple hasbeens, for they retreated up the canyon, with us following. When they had gone as far as they could go, they turned and galloped toward us.

The horses were only trying to get past us, but we were scared witless. Harris screamed for my grandmother, who was three or four miles away. I was saving my breath for another burst of speed if necessary. We got out of the way to one side, and the horses galloped past. We quivered around for a while, then discarded the applecores and gave up on horse-catching for that day. By the time I was ten we knew a bit more about horses, and were more successful at catching them. A man who worked here and there in the area had left his horse with my grandfather for a year or two and we rode him almost daily. This advanced us considerably beyond burro-riding and catching horses with applecores.

How long ago that was, and how things have changed. Thinking back on those days, it seems like the memory of another epoch, a different century. Knowing how different things once were in my own lifetime has made it easier to get a feeling for how people lived and felt in remote historical eras. It has also aroused my curiosity about other times, other places.

When I was away from the homestead later, I often thought of the rambles Harris and I had taken, the early days when there were cattle on the range, and the cowboys we occasionally saw. But the postwar decline in cattle prices, together with the drouth, ended that way of life. We hoped that those days would return, but they were gone forever.

In a way that area was a microcosm or vestige of the nineteenth-century open range era in Texas and elsewhere. Cowmen in those days before barbed wire needed only enough land for a ranch head-quarters, corrals, and horse pasture, for their stock ran loose on state land. In our area half a dozen families lived on 160-acre homesteads, where they had fenced a small pasture for keeping a saddle horse and perhaps a team. The remainder of the land was open range, where their cattle and horses roamed freely.

As in the old days, all of the cowmen threw in together at round-up time, branded calves the way it had been done in Texas, and rounded up steers to sell in the fall. The range stayed open after the cowmen sold their cattle and left, but there were only abandoned horses on it, and in a few generations they ran at the sight of a man. Being there before the cattlemen left and having at least a glimpse of one of their open range roundups and other cow work gave me a feeling for that part of the West that vanished with the coming of barbed wire.

When the cowmen sold off their cattle during the 1920s there were a few renegade steers that hid out alone and were warier and harder to catch than coyotes. A few times Harris and I were fortunate to be at the right place to watch the cowboys catch some of them. We kept out of sight, for they didn't think highly of dirt-farmer homesteaders or their brats, and they'd have run us off if they'd seen us.

One big red steer was especially difficult to catch, and it was only after much hard riding and exquisite swearing that they got him into a small pasture enclosed by a barbed wire fence. We watched it all from the limb of a giant juniper tree about a quarter of a mile away.

After the steer was in the pasture the cowboys rode off to get a truck to haul him out. We kept watching the steer for a while. It was a magnificent, muscular animal, as quick and alert as a Miura bull in a Spanish bullring. Suddenly it tossed its head, gave a bellow, and headed for the fence in a dead run. It was a fairly high fence; as he cleared it one hind hoof snapped the top strand of wire.

The cowboys were pretty disgusted when they returned and found him gone. They expressed their feelings in colorful and descriptive terms, which seemed to have a therapeutic value for them, for when they finished swearing they pulled down their hats and followed his tracks into the hills. When they finally caught him again they tied his head up tightly against a piñon tree and left him to contemplate his sins while they went after the truck.

I don't know if I clung to memories more than Harris or anyone else did, but I certainly did my share of daydreaming, much of it about horses. For Harris and me, owning horses was our greatest ambition.

School Bus Days

Before Los Angeles County began bussing us country children to Little Rock for school, we had a year of schooling in an unoccupied house. Then the county hired Gus Guenther to haul us to Little Rock. He had a Ford truck on which he built a rectangular body with benches along both sides and across the back. The sides were open from about midway to the top; this made it a bit cool in the winter, but gave us a good view of the countryside.

We lived closest to the mountains of all the kids who rode the bus, so we were the first to be picked up each morning and the last to get home at night. We were at the end of a two-track road about two miles off a graded dirt road that the county maintained. About all that meant was sending out a couple of men with mule teams and scrapers to remove the worst bumps and fill the holes or washouts. It was eleven miles to Little Rock, but the bus had to go all over the place and up a lot of rutted roads to collect its load of urchins, so the trip was a lot longer than eleven miles. Most of us carried our lunches in rectangular metal tobacco boxes.

We rode that bus all through grammar school except occasional years when we were with my mother in Berkeley and one year when she taught school in Shasta County. Most of the time I looked out of the open sides, hoping to see cowboys or range horses.

One morning one of the LePage girls gave everyone, including Gus, the driver, some little flat, square pieces of candy. We rarely tasted candy, so we eagerly devoured all that came our way. We noticed that the little squares had what appeared to be a foreign name stamped on them. None of us knew any Latin, so we agreed that the candy's name was probably in that language.

That morning the ride to school seemed longer than usual, the road much bumpier, and Gus was pushing the old bus faster than ever. When he brought it skidding to a stop at the school he turned the switch and was the first one out, trotting toward the outbuildings behind the school. Every waif on the bus, except the one who had been so generous with her candy, was grimly heading in the same direction although we couldn't keep up with Gus. Except that there were no happy faces among us, we might have looked like the Pied Piper and the children of Hamlin. The candy-giver ambled after us, smirking and tittering. Later we learned that the name on the candy wasn't Latin at all. ExLax was just one of those made up words, but one we didn't soon forget.

One day we did see cowboys holding an open range roundup. To me it was thrilling, and I'd have mortgaged my future to stay there and watch. At one side was a fire to heat the branding irons. While a bunch of cowboys held the herd, a couple of skillful ropers circled it and deftly roped the calves. They dragged the calves toward the branding fire, with the cows bawling after them. We had a good look at them, for the road wound around the holding area. These cowboys also put on a rodeo at Llano, and we got to see that. About all I remember of it was that a steer roper's cinch or latigo strap broke after he'd roped a steer. He sat in his saddle on the ground, dug in his heels, and held the steer until his partner heeled it.

Llano was a utopian colony that flourished for a time, but when the drouth came and the water supply dwindled, they had to leave. Years later, when I was a graduate student at Berkeley, I ran across an article about the colony. I think it said that the people moved to Louisiana and started over again. Llano became a ghost town; gradually the houses were dismantled and removed until little trace of it remained.

Once when the school bus was going up the rutted road through the junipers toward the homestead, Gus suddenly applied the brakes. In the road ahead of us was a huge red bull with lowered head and thick horns. He gave the bus an ugly look and low, challenging bellow. He pawed the earth, raised and lowered his head a few times, and looked as if he was getting ready to charge. The bus was also red, and the bull may have been trying to figure out its sex so he could decide whether to mate with it or bowl it out of his way. We watched breathlessly for what seemed a long time before the powerful animal decided he had other business to attend to, and sauntered majestically away.

Those cattle were all wild and unsociable, and anyone on foot needed to stay near trees or fences. A story going around was of a boy on foot who was charged by a bull. He stood with his back against a tree until the last second, then leaped aside. According to the story the bull knocked himself silly, and the clever boy was a local hero. We all envied him his fame and hoped to emulate his feat, but fortunately never had the opportunity.

Over the years the growing drouth and falling beef prices forced the small ranchers to sell their stock, and in a few more years there wasn't a single cow to be seen on the range. There was no way to earn a living on those 160-acre homesteads in that region, as my grandfather demonstrated the rest of his life. One by one the cowmen and their families moved away, leaving some of their horses loose on the range. We often saw the horses from the school bus or on occasional trips to Little Rock, where my grandfather swapped sacks of corn and string beans for groceries. Several of the horses I still remember because of their striking colors. One was an iron gray or blue roan that really looked blue from a distance. Another was a buckskin mare, a rich golden yellow with contrasting black mane and tail and black from the knees down, like bays are. Both of these belonged to men still living in the area.

One year the buckskin mare had a red colt with a golden mane and tail, and legs of the same color. He had a broad blaze on his face that was spade-shaped at the top, and was muscular and beautiful. I named him Ace and dreamed of flying around the country on his back.

Occasionally we joined our mother for the school year at Berkeley or elsewhere, but usually returned to the homestead in summer. Being away from time to time caused me to lose track of some of the horses I admired, and Ace was one of them.

Both of our grandparents read every evening, and we kids read until bedtime. The county occasionally placed small branch libraries in people's homes, and for a few years there was one about three miles down the road from us. Most of the time the nearest one was in Little Rock. When it was close all of us walked down there every two weeks and each checked out two books.

We passed them around and usually we'd all read most of them before we took them back and checked out a new supply.

The branch library was one of the few meeting places available for us country folks, and it provided welcome opportunities to swap gossip. I recall pretending to be deeply engrossed in making a selection while two women discussed some young couple whose first child had arrived not many months, at least not the conventional number, after they were married. "Oh, they'd been playing with fire!" one said. The other nodded in enthusiastic agreement and with what seemed to me an expression that successfully combined disapproval with envy. I figured out what they were talking about, and must admit that I enjoyed it as much as they did.

My reading tastes in those days ran to Zane Grey, B. M. Bower, Clarence Mulford, and the like, although I read whatever was available when I ran out of these. Sir Walter Scott was another favorite. We had books of the poems of Longfellow and Kipling at home, and I memorized dozens of them, from "The Skeleton in Armor" to "Gunga Din."

At night we settled around the kitchen table, with a tall kerosene (we called it coal oil) lamp in the center. When my grandfather came home with a Coleman gasoline lantern it was a great improvement. I understand that rural electrification has reached that hinterland, but there wasn't any electricity within miles when we lived there.

Runaways

After we'd been on the homestead a few years all three of us talked a lot about going to Arizona. Once when I was six or seven we bundled up our most treasured possessions and slipped away. Lavon, who planned the escapade, left my grandmother a note telling her we were running away and going to Arizona. We followed a trail through the sandrocks to Valyermo, a big fruit farm that was, we were sure, in the same direction as Arizona. We trudged along until late afternoon, prattling about what we'd do when we got to Arizona and found our Aunt Mable.

When the sun got close to the horizon we glumly headed home by the road around the foothills instead of trying to follow the trail through the spooky sandrocks in the dark. By road the distance was five or six miles longer, and when it was absolutely dark we still had five miles to go. By that time the prattling had stopped; all three of us were wondering what sort of welcome we'd get when we finally reached the homestead.

From this distance in time it seems to have been a rather brainless, humorous affair, but not to my grandmother. For one thing, the idea of us trying to reach our father's family was outrageous and unforgivable, not to mention the worry we'd caused her. "You ungrateful brats!" she said, by way of welcome, looking as stern as an executioner. "Gene, where's the switch?" He handed her one he'd cut earlier, a length of willow about the thickness of his thumb, one that wouldn't bend when laid on with a will. "You were probably at the bottom of this, Emmet," she said to me, so I got the first turn, before her arm grew tired. She had more to say between whacks, but I was squalling from pain while Lavon and Harris made a chorus in anticipation, and I couldn't hear the whole message.

Quite a few years later she needed medical treatment and went to Los Angeles to stay with our Aunt Isabelle. Lavon was in Berkeley with our mother, and Harris and I stayed on the homestead with our grandfather. We were still determined to go to Arizona, but planned to go on horseback this time.

We set out one morning with little preparation and no food. Rex and Princess were somewhere on the range, but we couldn't find them. That slowed us some and caused a change of plans; instead of riding we set out across the desert on foot. We trudged along until dark, having had nothing to eat since breakfast. When the sun set it turned cold. We scraped out trenches for sleeping in a sandy spot, but most of that long night we shivered and listened to coyotes yipping and other nocturnal voices of the desert.

The next day we decided we'd better go back and try to find some grub and the horses. It's curious about going without food that long; the only times we felt hunger were at the customary hours of meals. Between those hours the hunger went away. Late in the afternoon, by accident, we saw A. P. Aldrich driving along the dirt road toward us. We tried to hide, but he'd seen us. He talked us into going with him to wherever he was working, and got the cook to give us several man-sized helpings of stew and biscuits. Then he and Curly Morrow took us back to the homestead, to be sure my grandfather didn't apply his peculiar brand of chastisement to us. Curly Morrow said he'd be glad to take us off our grandfather's hands, but that wasn't necessary; he didn't raise any row. Harris and I went back to our dreaming.

Harris and I owed A. P. Aldrich a debt of the kind one can never repay, for he was the nearest thing to a father we knew. He had a little homestead on some leftover hilly land that could support a few milk goats and nothing more. He had to work somewhere all of the time, but kept a few goats, a team of mules, and a little saddle horse named Gus. He hunted deer and trapped coyotes in the winter, so he, Ruby, and their son Ralph managed to scrape by, which was about all that most people were able to do in that area.

For us he was a surrogate father, the one person we could always talk to about anything. Without him our lives would have been much lonelier and emptier. Once he told us, "You boys were made to excel at something. I don't know what it might be, but I'm sure of it." Those words meant more to us than any others, for our grandmother was sure we'd amount to little and didn't keep it a secret. A. P.'s expression of confidence in us, whether genuine or out of kindness, did more for us than he may have imagined.

A. P. insisted on being called by his initials, for he'd been named after his grandfathers, Aaron and Penrose. A. P. A., he said, stood for American Pack Animal. He was a tease and had a great sense of humor. He'd been a cowboy at one time and he knew a lot of the old cowboy songs. He was a near-hero to us.

I lived with A. P. and his family on weekdays for part of one year when I was attending the high school in Lancaster, about thirty-five miles away. They were living in one of the houses on the old West ranch that had been abandoned when the water supply declined, and the school bus was parked in the barn there. The driver lived up near the mountains, and the part of the year I lived at the homestead I had to meet him about two miles away. That meant leaving home at six in the morning and walking the two miles. Those days I didn't get home until seven at night.

A Walk in the Snow

In midwinter one year when I'd been at school in Berkeley my grandmother and the three of us rode the train from Berkeley to Palmdale. I mentioned to one of my teachers that I had to leave school and return to my grandfather's ranch. That seemed to ring a bell: he asked me a lot of questions about horses and such. I must have supplied the right answers, for he told the class about it. That made me a one-hour celebrity; the students called me "Cowboy," which I relished, and all appeared a bit envious — a new experience for me. Here I was, leaving right in the middle of the school year, and I'd soon be galloping over the range on a half-wild horse. To them it must have sounded deliciously romantic.

That wasn't the way it would be by a whole lot, but I enjoyed the attention too much to destroy their illusion. Actually I'd be riding a school bus, not a horse, for the rest of the year. Maybe during the summer Harris and I would find an abandoned horse we could ride, maybe not.

Returning to the homestead was always exciting, even though it meant an abrupt change for us. We'd gotten used to city life, having close neighbors, schools and libraries within walking distance,

35

electric lights, gas stoves, and indoor plumbing. All of that would be left behind once we passed through the gap in the foothills to the isolated homestead up against the mountains. But the old place had gotten the same sort of hold on me that Arizona had; it generated more memories than any other place. Coming back to it each time was in a way going back to our roots, a nostalgic adventure in becoming reacquainted with everything remembered. This trip, as it turned out, was not a typical going home for us.

I can't recall what caused us to go back to the homestead at that time of year, but it must have had something to do with my mother's financial situation. My grandmother had written to tell my grandfather to meet us at the station, as usual. The train pulled into Palmdale about three in the afternoon; I looked out, hoping to be the first to spot my grandfather and his old Ford truck, but couldn't see either. We dragged our old suitcases off the train and looked everywhere for him, but he wasn't to be found. The truth was we were stranded twenty miles from the homestead and we didn't remember a single person in Palmdale.

Fortunately I did remember that the high school bus from Lancaster let some kids off in Palmdale before heading for Little Rock and on to our neck of the woods. We waited where it usually stopped. It came along about four o'clock, and the driver said he'd take us as far as he could. I guess we were all wondering what had happened to my grandfather, but my grandmother looked grimmer than usual, so we rode the whole way in silence.

The sun had already set and it was dark when the driver let us off about two miles from the homestead. The ground was covered with several inches of snow, and in the starlight we could tell that no car had been over the rutted road since the snow had fallen. We trudged homeward in the dark, lugging our baggage, afraid of what we might find.

Lavon and I led the way, each walking in a rut, and my grandmother and Harris followed in our tracks. We were about halfway home when coyotes started yipping on our right.

"Do you think they might attack us?" Lavon asked me in a low voice.

"Naw," I replied, trying to sound as if I was absolutely sure. My arms ached from carrying a battered and heavy suitcase, but I plodded a bit faster.

Other coyotes started yipping on our left, and it sounded as though two packs were converging on us. Maybe they were famished enough to attack people. The fuzz on the back of my neck was already standing up; now it tried to walk away. I had learned to imitate coyotes, and here was a great opportunity to chat with them in their own language, but for some reason I wasn't tempted. Probably it was just two coyotes exchanging greetings or rabbit reports; coyotes have a way of sounding like five times as many. They seemed to be coming closer and closer, but they must have caught our scent, for they suddenly stopped.

When we finally came in sight of the cabin we saw a faint glow of light at the window; my grandfather was sitting at the kitchen table reading. It had been so cold for two weeks that he hadn't been able to crank up the truck, he said, so he hadn't gotten the mail and didn't know we were coming. He was quietly apologetic, which for him was an unfamiliar role.

World's Champion Coyote Yipper

In summer on the homestead Harris and I, and sometimes our cousins from Los Angeles, slept outside under the stars, and I don't recall that we ever got rained on. At forty-five hundred feet above sea level the nights were cool and the air clear. We watched meteors — shooting stars, we called them — and went to sleep to the sound of coyotes yipping. I got to be able to imitate coyotes quite convincingly, but after a few successful performances I concluded that public exhibitions could be risky.

The first time I knew my imitation was effective was when I was heading home from somewhere on the two-track road through the junipers. I heard Harris and our cousin Alan, who was about his age, chattering along toward me. I hid and gave them a few yips, thinking Harris would no doubt recognize my voice.

"Aw, it's just an ole coyote," Harris said, and they both shouted to scare it off. When the yipping continued and grew louder, they got scared.

"Maybe it's a wolf!" Alan exclaimed. There'd never been wolves in that part of the country, but that did it. They started off on the run, when I called and stopped them.

"You sure had us fooled," Harris admitted. I had to agree that it was a pretty good act.

Occasionally we hoofed it down to the mail route, where there was a community mailbox. It was about five miles away, and mostly uphill coming back, so we didn't check for letters often. One time we were waiting for the mail truck to come when we saw a woman and her two little girls walking down the road toward us. We hid in the bushes up the hill behind the mailbox and waited. When they were about fifty feet from the box I gave them the coyote treatment. They stopped.

"Scat, you cowardly coyote!" the woman shouted, but when the yipping continued they almost panicked. We started talking loudly then, so they'd know the coyotes were the two-legged kind. The woman said some pretty mean things about us, and she had a surprisingly rich vocabulary, though in a cussing match with my grandfather she'd have been a poor second. We kept out of sight, for if they'd recognized us and told my grandmother, I'd have been in trouble.

The last time I coyoted anyone wasn't all fun. I was wandering around as usual, and saw a car alongside the road and two couples sitting under a tree eating lunch. I was hungry as usual, and thought they might not know much about coyotes. If they got scared and left in a hurry they might overlook a sandwich or two. So I circled round them in the junipers and sang them a coyote song. It worked perfectly—the women squealed and hopped into the car, and I started thinking about the sandwiches they must have abandoned. About that time one of the men pulled a rifle out of the car.

"He's right over there behind that tree," the other man said, pointing to my hiding place. The man with the gun fired a shot that thudded into the tree. I started running and yelling at the same time, zigging and zagging for all I was worth, and scared absolutely witless. He kept shooting, and it sounded like an elephant gun or some kind of cannon he was using. The whine of a bullet as it ricocheted off a rock a few yards away I found as stimulating as the roar of the rifle.

"It's a big coyote!" the other man yelled. "Shoot him!" I knew I sounded like a coyote, though I was sure I didn't look like one, but the more I yelled and waved my arms the more he shot at me. It seemed like a lifetime before I was over a ridge and out of his sight, although it couldn't have been more than a few seconds, for I was making pretty good tracks. I figured I'd been so convincing that even when they saw me they thought they were seeing a coyote. I'd gotten so good at imitating coyotes that it was downright dangerous. I kept running for several miles, and didn't stop until my skinny legs protested. They kept twitching even after I stopped.

I didn't tell anyone about my close call except Harris; although it was probably my most convincing performance and an unforgettable experience, I didn't feel like bragging about it.

The next time we went to the general store at Pearblossom the storekeeper looked at me over his spectacles. "Can you imitate coyotes?" he asked.

I was tempted to admit I was probably the world champion at imitating coyotes, but something told me this was a time for modesty. He usually ignored us kids, and I couldn't think of any reason he'd want to know about my only talent.

"No," I replied. "The only thing I can imitate is a buzzard." Buzzards don't make any sounds that I ever heard.

"A couple of men were here the other day. Said some blond kid tried to scare them by barking like a coyote. He had 'em fooled until they started shooting at him with a twenty-two, then he really split the wind. They were still laughin' when they stopped here. I thought mebbe it was you."

"Wish I'd seen it," I lied. "Must've been funny." Right then I knew for sure the world wasn't ready for my coyote act.

Round Mountain

In 1925 my mother took a teaching job in a one-room schoolhouse in the woods near Round Mountain, a village in Shasta County in northern California. She was a student at the University of California and needed to earn some money to continue. There were six other children in the school; she got the job, she said, because she could increase the enrollment to nine. The three of us were put on the train and she met us in Berkeley. We took a big bag of sandwiches for sustenance and slept in our seats. The train went through Santa Barbara early in the morning after a big earthquake, and we saw brick chimneys all over the sidewalks. To cross San Francisco Bay in those days, trains were uncoupled and pushed onto ferryboats.

From Redding we took a bus (they called it the stage) to Round Mountain, where some people met us and took us to the farmhouse where we were to live. It had a small orchard, a barn, and a pasture. A lady gave the new schoolmarm a horse named Jack, a McClellan army saddle, harness, and a buggy. This was fortunate, for the general store in Round Mountain was three miles away.

Jack hadn't been ridden for a while, and he was spirited and frisky. I was ten and hadn't ridden enough to feel confident, so it took me a while to get brave enough to ride him. He was perfectly well behaved and just wanted some action. I rode him all over the country after that. Once it was nearly dark and we were several miles from home. I was standing alongside him dawdling, and he knew it was time to head for the barn. He turned his head and gave me a push toward the saddle, and when I climbed on he galloped all the way home.

The snow was so deep there in winter that they ran the school through the summer and had vacation in the winter. The county paid some student eight dollars a month to sweep the floor each morning and ring the bell ten minutes before eight o'clock. Most of us got a turn at it, and that eight dollars was the first money I ever earned. I bought a pair of cheap spurs and some other items out of a mail-order catalog.

The country was mostly wilderness, with a few farms and ranches scattered about. The range cattle were pretty wild, and it took hard-riding cowboys to corral them. I followed along at every opportunity but usually got left far behind if they were chasing a steer. One time a neighbor who had a farm across the road from us announced that he had seen a "bear card" in our orchard. We looked all over the place for bears or cards but saw only some chewed apples and a pile of manure.

Somehow I had skipped the second grade. Ages and grades weren't paired in country schools in those days, and when I was supposed to be in the fifth grade in Little Rock I was put in the sixth. I think it must have been in the fifth grade that they taught how to parse sentences, for I was never exposed to that exercise. It didn't sound like something I couldn't live without, so I never bothered to learn it.

At Round Mountain I was supposed to be in the seventh grade, but because Lavon and Alice Bishop were eighth graders, I was put with them for convenience. At the end of the year the eighth graders were given a county-wide examination to see if they should go on to high school or have another year in grammar school. My mother said I might as well take the test for practice. It must have been easy, for to the surprise of all the report was that I'd passed.

When the school year ended we went back to the homestead while my mother returned to Berkeley. It was winter and school was in session, so we had no vacation that year, which I considered an outrage. I went back into the eighth grade. The next year we were in Berkeley, where it was decided, correctly, that I was still too young for high school, so it was back into the eighth grade for the third time. By then I was thoroughly bored with school and didn't do much homework or anything else for several years, and it's a wonder I was ever accepted into college.

First Levis

One of the things that made our stay in Round Mountain really memorable for me was that my mother bought me my first pair of Levis there. I don't know how long Levis in boys' sizes had been available, but to me they were a milestone toward manhood, like your first shave, or when your voice got through changing and cracking.

The reason this was so significant to me was that I knew all real cowboys wore Levis, rolled up a couple of inches at the bottom of the legs. Cowboys, of course, also wore high-heeled boots and sombreros and chaps. Somewhere I had acquired an old N. Porter Saddle and Harness Company catalog from Phoenix, and had pored over it until I wore it out. I drooled over the photos of hats, chaps, boots, saddles, and spurs. I knew it would be a long time before I could hope to own such things, but Levis were a major step in that direction.

If we'd worn regular pants the change to Levis might not have been so momentous. But my grandfather had been a carpenter before he became a homesteader, and he always wore bib overalls. No cowboy, whether self-respecting or not, would be caught alive in bib overalls, but that's what my grandfather always bought us. So it was wear them or nothing.

That's why getting my first pair of Levis was like winning a range war against rustlers or land-grabbers. I was proud to wear them; they reminded me of the verse in "The Strawberry Roan" that goes: "I was standin' round town, just spendin' my time, Out of a job and not earnin' a dime, When a stranger steps up, and says I suppose, You're a bronc ridin' man, by the cut of your clothes."

I wore the first pair of Levis until I grew clear out of them, and never again wore bib overalls. I developed an attachment to Levis that was almost an addiction. More than half a century later I still wear Levis almost every day, not the wide-bottom kind but the old straight leg ones with copper rivets.

Riley

Once I rode Jack through the woods and down a trail that I hadn't seen before in my wanderings. In a little clearing by a big weeping willow stood a cabin, a corral, and a shed. Jack stopped and I was sitting on him looking around, wondering who lived there, when I suddenly became aware that a man was standing in the cabin doorway. My scalp tingled and my hair tried to stand straight up, for he was an Indian and was holding a rifle. We stared at each other for a moment. His face was impassive but I'm sure mine must have showed shock, maybe even terror.

He smiled, and I felt a sensation of relief sweep over me clear to my toes. "Put your horse in the pen, son, and come in," he said. "I was just oiling my rifle."

I put Jack in the corral with a roan Indian pony and went into his one-room cabin. There were a couple of deerskins on the floor and some antlers nailed to the wall. He had a small wood stove, a cot in one corner, and several handmade stools.

"They call me Riley," he said. I told him my name. By then I was relaxed, thrilled to meet a real Indian, especially one who was friendly to stray urchins. He told me the Indian name of his tribe, but I've forgotten it.

"There used to be a lot of us," he said softly. "Now there aren't many of us left."

We went outside. "See that tree?" He nodded toward the weeping willow. "When I first came here ten years ago that was my riding whip. I stuck it in the ground. Look at it now." We talked a bit longer, then it was time for me to go.

"Come back any time you can," he told me. "If I'm not here, go on in and sit a while. I probably will be back soon."

I visited him at every opportunity. We walked for hours among the pines and firs, miles from where anyone else lived. We saw springs and grassy places where deer grazed. His hearing was keen and his eyes didn't miss a thing. He showed me deer tracks. "Can you tell me which are buck tracks?" he asked. I couldn't. "Bucks are heavier than does. Their toes spread a little from the weight. See." He showed me the difference.

"Can you tell which are the freshest?" I had no idea. We knelt and he pointed to almost invisible signs that told him which were the oldest and which the most recent. Once after that we surprised a buck and two does that quickly disappeared into the forest.

"You know these tracks are fresh," Riley said. "Study them so you'll be able to recognize fresh tracks next time you see them." Some of the tracks were in mud; others were in soft earth, sand, and grass. I looked them all over carefully, but wasn't at all sure I saw everything he did. We returned an hour later and looked them over again. Those in the mud had dried a little where the mud was thin. The tracks in the sand were beginning to lose their clear-cut shape. I had a bit more difficulty seeing any change in the ones in soft earth. At first I couldn't see any sign of tracks in the grass, but Riley patiently squatted down and pointed to stems that were slightly bent or broken. An hour later he could still point out faint traces as the grass was slowly straightening up.

Other times we'd go deep into the woods and sit silently for hours, listening to the sounds and watching for wild animals. Riley knew all about the habits of wild creatures. Although in school my attention span was limited, I never wearied of Riley's teaching.

One day we were in the woods about half a mile or more from his cabin when he stopped and seemed to be listening. "I think I have visitors coming," he said, and we walked back to his cabin. Two Indian couples rode up about the time we arrived. I never found out whether Riley heard something I hadn't heard or had some special sense. The two men were dressed like cowboys; the women wore long, colorful skirts. They spoke to Riley in their own language, dismounted, and put their ponies in his corral. I knew they hadn't come to see me, so I hopped on Jack and left.

Another time Riley gave me a half-coyote pup that had been caught in a trap. One front paw was swollen, and Wolf, as I named him, always limped thereafter.

Wolf

Wolf and I became inseparable; he went everywhere with me, even to the little one-room school. I couldn't take him inside, but he waited near the door for recess and lunch times, when we acted as if we hadn't seen each other in days. I talked to him a lot and he seemed to understand my mood if not my words. When I felt low he sensed it and licked my hand to cheer me up. The only times he seemed moody were when I had to leave him. He was a real one-boy dog; he tolerated the rest of the family but didn't shower them with affection. He grew into a handsome animal, with alert, pointed ears and bright eyes.

When we left Round Mountain to return to the homestead, and my mother went back to Berkeley to continue her studies, we took the bus to Redding, about forty miles away. There we boarded the train for Palmdale, taking a big sack of sandwiches to last us the day-and-a-half trip. We had to muzzle Wolf and let him ride in the baggage car. He made the journey without difficulties but he wasn't happy about being muzzled.

Soon Harris and I were tramping all over the country, revisiting all of our favorite haunts, with Wolf limping along at my side. People we saw in our wanderings admired Wolf and remarked on his attachment to me. Naturally I was proud of him, and it boosted my ego to be the object of his affection and loyalty. Ego-boosters and affection were scarce in those days. When I got off the school bus Wolf was always waiting to greet me, as overjoyed to see me as I was to see him.

A year later, at the end of summer, my mother decided that the three of us should join her in Berkeley for the school year. We were always excited about train trips, whether heading for Berkeley or returning to the homestead. But I would have preferred to stay on the homestead and continue my rambles with Wolf, and occasionally getting to ride a horse. I didn't want to go at all when I learned that I couldn't take Wolf.

When the time came for us to leave he sensed that something was wrong from the glum way I was acting. I hugged him for the last time, blinking back tears, while he looked at me questioningly, almost reproachfully, licking my face as if he knew I was deserting him. I had a lump in my throat when I climbed in the back of the old truck for the ride to the railroad station at Palmdale.

Not long after we got to Berkeley my grandmother wrote that Wolf had disappeared. My grandfather had tried to find him; people had seen him everywhere we'd gone together. They tried to feed him and coax him to stay, but he sniffed around for a while then limped off to continue his search. When this letter came I rushed out of the house and took a long walk in the Berkeley hills, for I didn't want anyone to see me bawl.

Berkeley

I don't remember what year it was that Harris and I first went to Berkeley to stay for the school year, but I was in junior high; La-von was already there. For Harris and me it was all strange and wonderful — electric lights, streetcars, and all kinds of autos other than Model T Fords. A ride on a streetcar cost seven cents, and you could get a transfer and continue on another route. We lived in the Berkeley hills in the last house on Panoramic Way, which wound back and forth up the hill. For pedestrians there were concrete steps, more than a quarter of a mile of them, and that's the way we came and went. At first we thought nothing of walking clear down to the bay to watch men fishing off the piers, although it was three or four miles away. It's embarrassing to remember what country yokels we were, greener than alfalfa. During those years my mother supported us with whatever she earned as a teaching assistant along with any other work she could get in the astronomy department. It was a hand to mouth existence, but we weren't familiar with any other kind.

On Saturday morning we'd trudge down to the Piggly Wiggly store on Telegraph Avenue, then head back uphill with armloads of groceries. Sometimes we bought meat at the Berkeley Market. When I returned to Berkeley in 1939 to enter graduate school, I stopped at the Berkeley Market and saw that some of the same men were still there. "I'll never forget your brother," one told me. "He used to come in after school with an ice cream cone, buy a dill pickle and a piece of cheese, and go out eating all three."

We all had library cards and I read everything the Berkeley Public Library had on the Apaches, probably because many of the bands were Arizona Indians. I was a lot more interested in the Apaches and their history than in any course in school.

Although my school work in junior high in Berkeley was nothing out of the ordinary, it was there that I had my first publication. The teachers selected a few stories to be published in the yearbook.

I had written a silly story that featured one of my current heroes — Ivanhoe. I had read it and other Scott novels by then and enjoyed them. I don't remember much about the story I wrote except that Ivanhoe made a daring escape and rescued someone, undoubtedly a distressed damsel. To my absolute astonishment it was chosen to be included in the yearbook. We couldn't afford to buy one, but I did get to see my very first publication, and fiction at that. Even at that stage I often thought I'd be a writer some day, I guess because I enjoyed reading so much. Perhaps the Ivanhoe story made me think that becoming a writer was a real possibility. I don't list it among publications, awards, and things like that which help to make one's *curriculum vitae* look long and at least superficially impressive.

Nearly sixty years later I turned from history to writing historical novels. Since my first effort was what might loosely be considered historical fiction, I have either completed the circle, as they say, or entered second childhood.

Ace

One weekend after we'd returned to the homestead from Round Mountain Harris and I were out looking for a horse we knew we could catch. We found it with several others in an abandoned corral and managed to close the gate before they saw us. One of the horses was Ace, the red one with golden mane and tail I'd admired as a colt. He'd been broken to ride, I was sure, but apparently he'd been running on the range for a while because he was nervous and boogery. I was determined to catch him.

That took about an hour. I kept approaching him carefully until he finally let me pet him and tie a rope around his neck. He was quivering, and I was afraid he'd explode any minute, so I was as nervous as he was. I led him home, then put a bridle on him and finally got up nerve enough to climb on. I was scared, and I didn't get on right after bridling him. When I finally got up the courage to get on, all he did was to cock an ear back at me.

I rode him all over on weekends for the next month or two, and every day when school was out. We had no saddles, but were accustomed to riding bareback. Ace was gentle but jumpy and easily startled; when he shied at something he went sideways about fifteen feet. After I discovered that, I could stick to him like his own skin and figured I was getting to be a pretty fair rider.

Ace and I got along as if we were made for each other. It wasn't long before he was easy to catch; in fact, he would start coming toward me when I called him. I didn't teach him that — he learned it on his own. He'd stand there looking at me, bobbing his head up and down like a wild stallion for better focus, then start walking toward me.

One day a car drove up, which was unusual, for we didn't have many visitors unless someone made a wrong turn and needed directions. A man and a woman were in the car. When the man got out I saw he was wearing a Stetson and cowboy boots and looked like a prosperous rancher. He asked me if I'd seen a red horse, and I knew they'd come for Ace. I bit my lip to keep it from quivering, then told him the horse was on our pasture. My voice sounded strange, as though I had a cold.

The woman got out of the car. She apparently was one of those who came up from Los Angeles to spend summers over at Big Rock, where there was a lodge and stables and trout fishing in Big Rock Creek. I figured she must own Ace, but didn't ask her, for she said nothing to us. It was difficult to tell if she even saw us, for she acted as if we weren't there. Harris and I just looked at each other, then at our bare feet.

The man took a saddle and bridle out of the car and set them on the ground. Then he got out a lariat and shook out a loop. "Always have to rope him when he's been loose for a while," he told the woman. "After a week or two he's easier to catch."

"You don't need to rope him," I said. "I'll catch him for you." He ignored me.

We walked to the pasture gate. The man looked around for a place to pen Ace so he could rope him. I took a short rope and headed down the trail until I saw Ace and the other horses across the dry creek. I called to him and went to meet him as he walked toward me. He nuzzled me as usual while I put my arms around his neck and fought back tears, knowing I wouldn't see him again. I led him back and handed the rope to the man. He and the woman exchanged glances but neither spoke. The man saddled Ace then climbed on to be sure he'd behave.

He dismounted and handed the reins to the woman. "There's a ranger trail through the sandrocks to Valyermo," I told her. "I can show you the way, and it's about eight miles shorter than going by the road."

She didn't reply, but looked at the man. "I don't know that trail," he told her. She turned Ace and trotted off down the road. The man got in his car and followed. Harris and I watched until they were both out of sight. I felt as though the world had come to an end.

I did see Ace once after that, several years later. I was riding through a grove of sycamore trees along Big Rock Creek on the way to Llano when I saw something red on the ground about a quarter of a mile away. I rode over to have a closer look. It was Ace, stretched out on the ground with a bullet hole between the eyes. Who shot him or why we never knew, but there were a lot of idiots with rifles who came up from the city on weekends, and some of them liked to shoot at any living animal.

Rex

Of all the horses I have ever owned or ridden, Rex has always had a special place in my affections and memories. There was a big bay mare that someone had abandoned on the range, and she was often around our place. I think my grandfather worked her some, though she was hard to catch.

One spring, when school was still in session, she was grazing around our place, and the next morning had a newborn colt by her side. Since I gave names to most horses I saw regularly, I named him Rex. And because he'd been born on our place, I looked on him as mine.

We saw the mare and colt frequently during the next two years. He was a powerful, good looking black as a two-year-old, with no white on him anywhere, and as wild as he could be. One weekend we managed to get him and the mare into our pasture. A couple of boys from Little Rock came by on Sunday morning, and we kept Rex running all day until we wore him down. About sundown I was able to get up to him and stroke his neck. I tied a long rope around his neck, and we pulled him around a little, although his sides were heaving, and he was really exhausted.

By then it was dark, and there was nothing more we could do for a week because of school. He dragged the rope all week and got used to it. When we got hold of the rope the following Saturday morning he dragged us around for a while before we got him stopped. We didn't rush things, for we were skinny little kids and scared. But we kept at it, and gradually won his confidence.

I don't remember how long this went on, but we could only work with him on weekends until school was out. We finally got him lead-broken, and then persuaded him to let us put a snaffle bit in his mouth. There was one place in the pasture where the ground was so soft that a horse's hoofs sank in it, and we led him there. We didn't own a saddle, so we tied a rope around his middle for a surcingle. Harris tried to hold Rex with a long rope while I climbed on. Somehow I screwed up my courage enough to hop onto his back. I could have held my breath for the whole ride and probably did, for I was soon on the ground. Harris couldn't hold him, but I was off before Rex left the soft ground, so I wasn't hurt. Just scared.

It gradually dawned on me that I didn't need to get thrown. We caught Rex and led him back to the same place and I climbed on again. That time I stayed with him, and when he bucked his way into the dry creek bed I didn't dare get thrown on all those boulders. Finally he got tired of bucking, ran for a time, then stopped.

Harris opened the gate and climbed on an old mare, and we started off down the road. Rex was quieter now, but still nervous and jumpy. I knew that if I got thrown out there on the range we might never catch him again, so I was as nervous as he was, but for a different reason. We rode to George Pallett's place, about three miles away, and fortunately didn't meet any cars on the road. Luckily for us George and Curly Morrow were both there.

George Pallett had come to Antelope Valley before World War I as a young cowboy with a herd of steers to fatten. He stayed with them all summer up near where the Los Angeles County Playground is today. There were few people in the valley at that time. He returned later and staked out a homestead with good soil and water, and his apple orchard made him one of the few in the area who got along quite well without having to work for others.

He had an old horse that had been born in Inyo County, a few hundred miles across the desert and up in the mountains. It was one of those "homing" horses one hears about occasionally. As long as it lived, any time a gate was left open the old horse headed across the desert for its home range. Many years later I used this concept of a homing horse in a children's book called *War Pony.*

We dismounted and talked a while. Both were friendly and helpful, and in a few words taught us a lot. Rex was obviously nervous and spooky, for he'd had grown up wild and didn't know much about people.

"Spit in his nostrils like the Indians did," Curly told me. "Then he'll know your scent and not be afraid of you." I did and it worked.

George Pallett handed me a burlap bag, a gunny sack in those days. "Son," he said, "hang onto him good so he doesn't break away from you, then throw this under him and over him until it doesn't bother him any more. That'll get him over being boogered by everything strange. It's another trick the Indians used." I followed his advice, and it worked, too. Rex was a lot easier to handle after that. Another trick Curly showed us was to tie a rope around a horse's neck, coil it, and tuck the coil under your belt. "If you get thrown," he said, "grab the rope and hang onto it while you're in the air. That way you can keep him from leaving the country." That proved to be a useful trick, not only for riding Rex but also on other wild ones we caught and broke. It kept me from having to walk home more than once.

There was a mule loose on the range for a time and my grandfather worked him some. Once we saw him when we were on the way home from Little Rock; my grandfather said he had some cultivating to do and for me to drive the mule in.

I hopped on Rex bareback as usual and went after him. I had to drive him four or five miles, and along the way he got a bit mulish at times. In exasperation I rode up close and whacked him on the rump with a short rope. He must have been equally exasperated, for he ducked his head and let fly with both hind hoofs. One of them caught me squarely on the shin. I flew through the air and landed on my back. Rex turned around and came back to me, as if wondering what I was doing there.

Before I climbed back on him I filled my pockets with small rocks. Rex and I stayed well out of range of flying hoofs, but whenever the mule gave me trouble I pelted him with rocks, wishing the while for a BB gun or something that would make more of an impression on him.

I rode Rex off and on for several years, I forget how many. Before I had him gelded he was almost a one-man horse, for he threw anyone else who tried to ride him.

A Visit from Father

An unexpected visit from my father was the most thrilling event of my life on the homestead. It was a total surprise, for I hadn't seen him since I was about four, my recollection of him had gotten hazy, and Harris didn't remember him at all. By this time we weren't even sure he really existed, for he was a subject we never discussed when our grandparents were present.

I had just started high school at the time, and to me it was the most adominable form of torture ever devised for young boys. I hated everything about it, from the two-mile walk at six in the morning to meet the school bus driver, to the meandering forty-mile ride to Lancaster. It was dark when I set out, it was dark when I got home at seven, and as far as classes were concerned, it was dark all day.

At high school in Lancaster I took the agricultural courses. We went on field trips to see all manner of farming and ranching operations, from hog raising to beef and dairy cattle. Many of the boys lived in the area around Lancaster, which is extremely fertile desert country, needing only water to be highly productive.

Some boys got started raising cattle on a small scale by purchasing newborn calves at dairies. Bull calves cost three dollars, heifers sold for five. If they had cows they raised the calves on milk; otherwise they fed them on powdered milk. Some had started with one calf, raised it and sold it, then bought more, and over a few years had the start of a small herd.

I was anxious to emulate them, and somehow scraped up three dollars to buy a day-old bull calf. I fed him night and morning on powdered milk, and had visions of him being the first of a growing herd. Then one night a late snowstorm struck, the temperature dropped, and I found my calf in bad shape. We bundled him up and got warm milk down him, and he hung on for a couple of days. With him went my dream of becoming a young cattleman, one more experience that seemed to tell me I was destined to be a loser.

All I ever thought about in that somber period was escaping and taking up the carefree life of a cowboy. My most cherished possessions were a few discarded Western story magazines that Harris and I took turns reading until we both knew the stories by heart.

Life seemed drab indeed, for our grandfather regarded our interest in horses as a lot of hereditary foolishness but not from his side of the family. To him it was nothing but an excuse to avoid honest toil like pulling weeds in the cornfield or cutting firewood, labors we knew were beneath any true son of the saddle.

We were mightily afraid of him, but that didn't stop us from slipping away at every opportunity to pester the few horses, wild or tame, that were still on the range. We were paid for these escapades occasionally by clouts on the head and kicks that wouldn't have gotten by the Marquis of Queensbury, but temptation to be with horses was something we could never resist. We caught horses and rode them in summer, but each winter we had to turn them loose, and sometimes months went by before we could catch them again. In the interim life was at a low ebb. It was at such a time that my father miraculously appeared.

A girl from the principal's office called me out of class one afternoon, and I was sure I was in trouble and was terrified. Although I usually covered my trail with reasonable success, at times I was lazy and careless, and there was always a chance of slip-up and exposure. I quickly began a mental catalog of recent transgressions as I reluctantly followed the girl to the office, but I couldn't think of anything I'd done that merited such a rich reward. Slow-witted as I was where school work was concerned, on occasions such as this my mind became surprisingly agile.

I wanted badly to ask her what the charge was so that I could muster a defense, but was afraid to. Instead I concentrated on creating an air of injured innocence. This might slow them up for a moment and give me time for fast thinking and a chance to spread confusion. I wasn't at all prepared for what she told me.

"Your father is here to see you," she said. I gasped.

"My father?" She nodded. She might as well have said it was the governor who wanted to see me. I followed her now without reluctance, but I was sure it must be a mistake. At least it wasn't a trap, and it might even be true.

It was. There he stood waiting for me, smiling pleasantly, well dressed and cleanshaven. I looked down at my faded chambray shirt, patched Levis, and painfully outgrown shoes that my grandfather had resoled with the tread of a blown-out tire. And some time after our mother's only brother had died our last name had been changed to Worcester. I didn't know if my father had been aware of that before he asked for me at the school, and was afraid he might have been embarrassed. Awkwardly I shook hands with him but found little to say.

"I've gotten you excused for the rest of the day," he said. "Show me the way out to the ranch so I can have a visit with Harris, too. He's still in grammar school, isn't he?"

We went out to his car, a late model Chevrolet coupe. Another thrill, for I rarely rode in anything but the despised school bus and my grandfather's ancient truck. We followed the paved highway to Palmdale before turning southeast toward the mountains. The bus always went by back roads most of the way to pick up children, and I seldom had a chance to see the stream of cars speeding northward from Los Angeles toward Tehachapi and Death Valley. My empty cup began to fill.

We didn't talk much on the ride to the ranch. I asked him where he was living, but his answer was vague. "Oh, I've been up in northern California for a while," he said. "Don't know where I'll settle next. May go back to Arizona." I felt a little numb.

When we came to the last four or five miles I kept watch for A. P.

Aldrich, for I was eager to have him see me with my father. Fortune beamed on me again. I spotted him riding near the road on Gus, his little black horse. "Please stop a minute," I said. "There's a man I want you to meet." He stopped the car and we got out. I waved to A. P., and he loped over to us. My big moment was at hand.

"A. P.," I said, "I want you to meet my father." I was bursting with pride, and I know it showed.

They shook hands and chatted for a few minutes, exchanging pleasantries to the effect that Harris and I were fine boys and other white lies and platitudes. Even though I was sure it wasn't true, I enjoyed it immensely; praise of any sort never escaped my grandfather. It was rarer than candy and much tastier.

We drove on so that he could have a short visit with Harris, who was as excited as I. Our grandparents were polite but cool. He stayed only about half an hour, and before he left he slipped each of us boys a quarter. We hadn't seen so princely a coin in years; I'd found a nickel one time but wasted it in a slot machine in Little Rock, thinking I would get a pack of chewing gum. I've never gotten over the bitter realization of my error when the wheels stopped spinning and nothing fell out. That experience gave me an undying distaste for gambling, so it probably was well worth the price. The quarters would be carefully hoarded for months.

As my father drove away, Harris and I stood and waved and watched long after the dust had settled. Now we had something to whisper about in secret, something to add variety to our store of dreams. Perhaps he would come again soon. Perhaps we could visit him. Perhaps. . . . We looked knowingly at each other, then noticed that our grandmother seemed wounded by our enthusiasm.

I didn't see my father again, for he never returned for another visit. We hoped and watched and waited and speculated endlessly as to which month, week, or day he might show up. Finally we grew forgetful and turned once more to chasing the elusive but real wild horses. In young boys hope doesn't spring eternal. It quickly withers and dies.

It was nearly twenty years later when I next heard of him. A much-forwarded letter caught up with me when I was in the navy shortly before the war ended. It was a curt letter from a lawyer in

Phoenix informing me that my father's will was in probate and, if I had any claims, to make them promptly. As I filed the letter away, unanswered, I thought again of that almost forgotten day when an immense boredom had been lifted and the world for the first time had suddenly seemed bright and hopeful. No claims, I thought. I spent my patrimony long ago.

The Hammerhead Kicker

One summer when I was twelve or thirteen we saw a tall, unbranded, ewe-necked, hammerheaded bay gelding running with some range horses. I remembered having seen him a few times before, and I figured that he was another abandoned horse. That's what he was, and for good reason.

At the first opportunity we ran him into a corral. He wasn't wild or difficult to handle, just unsociable as well as ugly. But he looked tough, like he could go all day and be ready for the next one. He was easy to bridle, so I was sure he'd been ridden. He didn't buck with me, but he hadn't had much training.

We rode about ten miles, and stopped by a spring for a drink of water and a rest. When I slipped off, that hammerhead quickly stepped forward, cocked his head around so he could take aim, and kicked me on the leg midway between knee and hip. I didn't weigh much, so I flew through the air, which probably saved me a broken leg. I had an excruciatingly painful knot on the little dab of muscle in my leg, but there was nothing to do but climb on and ride home.

When I got ready to dismount I pulled his head around so I could keep him from moving ahead and kicking me again. But I was still a scrawny, under-sized kid, and he was too strong for me to hold. He pulled loose and kicked me again, almost on the same spot. I was lucky he didn't break my leg, but I hobbled around for weeks after that.

Harris collected a pile of rocks by the gate. I led the outlaw to it and pulled the bridle off. We sent him on his way with a shower of compliments. If we'd had a gun with us we might have been eating horseburgers. It was only after this that I learned he had a bad reputation as a kicker. He always took aim and didn't let fly at random like most horses, and he never missed. He'd broken some legs, killed a dog or two, and had made himself generally undesirable. He was the worst kind of outlaw—tricky and deceitful.

When the summer was over and we were about to leave for Berkeley and school again, a man who lived up near the mountains four or five miles from us offered me a dollar to run the bay gelding into his corral. I'd done other things like that for him, always for the same dollar, and so far it was still in his pocket. I knew he wouldn't pay me this time, but for once I didn't care about that.

I drove the gelding into his corral and closed the gate. The man asked me if I thought the horse had been broken; I told him I was sure he'd been ridden some. He didn't offer to pay me, for I'd mentioned that we were leaving for Berkeley in a few days. It would have been worth a lot to me to have seen them tangle, for I knew what would happen. The horse would be deceptively easy to saddle and ride, and the man wouldn't be cautious the first time he dismounted. Old hammerhead would get one good shot at him, not two like he got at me. Then there'd be a settling of accounts, and I was sure that before it was all over each would have gotten something he deserved. A year or two later I asked him how the bay gelding had turned out. Apparently he'd suddenly gotten hard of hearing.

Desert Ride

One time when I was off wandering around the country alone, I came onto some range horses. One was a black mare with a bay filly that was a month or less old. The mare's brand was a backward S, so I knew she had belonged to a family that had left. They weren't wild, and I followed them to see if I could catch one. In going down a steep, gullied hill, the bay filly tumbled into a crevasse and couldn't get out, for she landed on her back.

I lifted her out and petted her a while, and we hit it off remarkably well. She followed me after that, and her mother followed her. With a bit of patience and coaxing, she followed me all the way back to the homestead. We called the mare Princess, and when the filly was weaned, we broke Princess to ride. The filly was a real pet, but her name escapes me.

One weekend when we were away, a couple of older characters from Little Rock came out and caught Rex and Princess and rode them home. They let the filly out, and she apparently followed them part of the way. The two men who took the horses said that they were range stock, and that they had as much right to them as we did. Since they were adults and we were skinny little kids, logic was on their side, and their theory was hard to refute.

Harris and I headed for Little Rock on foot, nevertheless, and we must have surprised them, for they said nothing when we climbed on Rex and Princess and left. We hunted all over for the bay filly, a yearling by this time, but we never found her. Either someone along the way had invited her in, or someone in Little Rock had her and didn't mention it to us.

When I was fourteen Harris and I decided to ride Rex and Princess from the homestead to Berkeley, which was about four hundred miles away. Our mother vicariously enjoyed such adventures, even though they seldom turned out as she anticipated. She thought it would be great to ride up past Mount Whitney and across the mountains at Tioga Pass. As it turned out we didn't get that far, fortunately for us, for at nine thousand feet, with only one blanket apiece, we'd have been miserably cold.

The first four or five days were spent crossing the Mojave Desert. We headed for Lancaster, then on to the town of Mojave. Then more desert on through Red Rock Canyon, which was where many a Western movie was filmed.

There was a big road crew camped there, building a highway through the canyon. In those days road-building was all done with human and animal labor, mainly horses and mules. Dirt was scraped up and moved and dumped with fresnos (big scoops pulled by teams), and road construction was a slow process. We visited with some of the teamsters, who seemed to think we probably were runaways, for they reminisced about youthful escapades of their own.

That night we camped in a corral the road-builders had used earlier, and which had enough hay scattered around in it to keep Rex and Princess content. The water in the creek was alkaline, and we and the horses had a hard time drinking it.

Late the next afternoon we saw a green spot up near the edge of the mountains, a mile or two from the highway. The green meant water, so we followed a trail there and found a spring, trees, and grass, a real oasis. But the water was full of alkali. The next day we crossed more desert to Little Lake, where the country seemed to be getting less arid and more interesting. About the only animals we saw, except for an occasional coyote or buzzard, were some wild burros, which disappeared on the run the moment they saw us.

At the Little Lake post office was a letter from my mother. She expected to take a teaching job in some other state, and we must turn back. Heading back across that expanse of desert was an unwelcome prospect, but we made it back to the spring, and the following day to the corral. Several ranchers stopped to ask if we'd seen anyone with horses. Apparently there had been a rash of horse stealing. This at least gave us something to talk about, like tracking down the wily thieves, recovering the stolen ponies, and the like. Riding hour after hour, day after day, across the desert got pretty monotonous, and we were glad to have something to talk about.

By the time we reached the corral where we had camped before, we were out of food and half-sick from alkaline water. The next morning we came to the road-builders' camp. One of the men who'd taken an interest in us before came to our rescue. He took us to the cook tent and had the cook rustle up a huge stack of pancakes for us, and he chatted with us while we devoured them. I think he figured that we'd found running away not all we'd expected, and were going home.

We made it back to the homestead a few days later, with nothing to eat at all for the last day or two. About that time we learned that we wouldn't be leaving California but would be in Berkeley at least another year after all.

Goodbye to the Homestead

After our ride across the desert and back I knew we would never return to the homestead to live, so I traded Rex to a friend of A. P.'s for a 1924 Chevrolet touring car. We could get driver's licenses at fourteen, and I already had one. We had a few dollars, which we figured was enough to get us and Collie to Berkeley. Gasoline was cheap, and we planned to sleep in a hayfield. If all went well we'd have enough for a hamburger or two. We made a couple of sandwiches that we shared with Collie; they were gone by noon.

We sailed happily along at about forty miles an hour, through Palmdale, Lancaster, and Mojave, then through the Tehachapis to Bakersfield. We talked about going back to the homestead someday to raise horses, and about other pipe dreams. In the afternoon we stopped at a service station to buy gas and wash some of the bugs off the windshield. A lean unshaven man in seedy looking clothes approached us.

"That's a handsome dog you boys have," he said, gesturing toward Collie. "How far are you boys going?"

I was wondering what his game was and whether or not we should tell him. "To Berkeley," Harris said.

"You've got room for another passenger," he said with a smile, showing his tobacco-stained teeth. "I need a ride to the Bay area. Mind if I join you?"

Harris and I looked at each other, but neither of us could think of a polite way of saying no. Later it came to me that I should have told him our mother forbade us to pick up hitchhikers and would take the car away from me if we did. By then it was too late.

He waved Harris into the back seat with Collie and climbed in beside me. At least he let me drive. As long as Collie was with us we weren't worried that he might try to get rough with us. When my mother pretended to hit one of us Collie gently took her wrist in his powerful jaws. If this turkey tried anything he'd be in for a surprise.

Before he joined us Harris and I had talked as we drove, creating our usual fantasies about what we would do next year or sometime in the future. Now we all rode in silence. The fun was over.

Late in the afternoon our unwanted passenger turned to me. "How much money do you have?" he asked.

"Just enough to buy gas," I told him.

"I haven't eaten since yesterday morning," he said. "See if you can spare six bits."

I parked the car outside a little cafe. He got a table near the window and kept an eye on us while we hungrily watched him gulp down bread, meat, and potatoes. We got out and walked around until we found a faucet so we could give Collie a drink. Then we let him put his initials on a few tires, and climbed back in the car. I felt sorry we couldn't feed him anything.

Our passenger ate quickly and was soon ready to travel. He burped a few times while our stomachs growled with hunger or in protest. Just before dark we saw a freshly mown alfalfa field and I drove the car off the road. We waited until our traveling companion had chosen his spot, then lay down about thirty feet from him.

That proved to be too close. As soon as it was quite dark he started talking to the Lord in a loud voice. This went on for a long time. Between his harangue and fighting off a few thousand mosquitoes that seemed as hungry as we were, getting to sleep was a problem. Harris and I lay there in misery, swatting at mosquitoes, whispering obscenities, and plotting painful and lingering forms of homicide for him.

The next morning we were all hungry, but there was no money left. Luckily we had gasoline enough to get us to Berkeley. When we drove past a pear orchard our passenger tour director must have had a revelation, for he ordered me to stop.

"Boys," he said, "I know the Lord won't mind if you pick up a few of those pears off the ground."

Harris and I looked glumly at each other. We knew he'd had a painfully long talk with the Lord the night before, but I couldn't remember anything being said about taking someone else's pears. We weren't sure, either, that the man who owned the orchard was tuned in to the Lord's thoughts on the subject, but we climbed over the fence and gathered a bunch of green pears off the ground. Our turkey friend let us take the risks then ate most of those hard, indigestible pears, for we found them inedible. All we could hope was that he'd get the green-apple quicksteps or worse. That would be some compensation.

When we got to Berkeley he acted as if he intended to stay with us. "You'll be in real trouble if you go home with us," I told him. "You'd better get out right here." I pulled over to the curb and he slowly got out. He stood there as though he was about to change his mind and rejoin us, but I let out the clutch and we sped off. He pretty much ruined what had started out as a fun trip.

That year my mother taught part-time at the university, while we went to high school. After skipping several grades and having to sit through the eighth grade two more times because I was too young for high school, I had totally lost interest and merely went through the motions of attending class. I swapped the Chevrolet for a Model T Ford roadster. The thing to do in those days was to undersling such jalopies, lowering the bodies four or five inches, which made them appear sporty and racy, at least in the eyes of the owners. A high school friend who was mechanically adept performed that operation on my Ford. I helped him whenever there was something that required strength rather than skill, but mostly kept him company while he did the work. I knew something about horses, but little about horseless vehicles. That situation hasn't changed much.

By the time we left Berkeley the next summer we had never been involved in any school activity outside the classroom, been to a party attended by girls as well as boys, or had girl friends. Still pretty much hayseeds, we had neither dress-up clothes nor the social graces to go with them, but I don't recall that we ever thought about such things.

Winter Park

In 1931 my mother accepted a teaching position at Rollins College in Winter Park, Florida. We piled into the 1928 Plymouth she'd bought and stopped overnight at the homestead to see our grand-parents. We saw our grandfather once after that, but our grand-mother died that year. We also stopped for a visit with Aunt Mable and family on the outskirts of Phoenix. I was more determined than ever that I'd return to Arizona one day.

Much of the trip was made on gravel roads, many of them just beginning to be paved. There were no motels on that route at the time, but many houses along the way had signs indicating that they took in travelers, and we always found a place to stay overnight. By the time we got within a few miles of Winter Park one evening, we were broke, for we wore out too many tires on those rough roads. Luckily for us, a woman who had rooms trusted my mother and put us up for the night. This was in the depths of the depression, and no one had much of anything. I remember a sign in a cafe that said, "Use less sugar and stir like hell; we don't mind the noise."

Winter Park was a new experience for us: we'd never run into seg-regation before. In the California schools we'd attended there had been a rich mix of races — Chinese, Japanese, Filipinos, blacks, and Hispanics — who participated freely in all activities. One year I'd shared a double desk with a black boy and had no reason to think that was unusual. Winter Park was a cultural shock, but living there one year didn't change our attitudes about racial matters. One night there was much excitement when hooded Ku Klux Klan members paraded through town and then crossed the railroad tracks to burn a fiery cross in the black section.

Seeing those hooded men out terrorizing blacks was a shocker to us. From the little I'd read about them, I knew that they also whipped and bullied whites who opposed them or whose conduct angered them. It was clear that any individual they went after — black or white — was helpless. They had safety in numbers, and law-men were presumably either with them or looking the other way. When we lived in Florida later I read about a group of them going after some Indians in South Carolina, the Lumbees, I think. The Indians got their rifles and shotguns, and a lot of white sheets were soon popping in the wind.

Like most institutions, Rollins was hard hit by the depression and for a time paid faculty members in scrip. We were there only until

Harris, Lavon, Mother, and Don, 1935

the summer of 1932, for my mother accepted a position in the astronomy department at Vassar College in Poughkeepsie, New York.
We still had Collie, and when we loaded up the Plymouth, neighbors came by to tell us how much they'd miss him. One woman who
adored him told us that once she'd tried to come to our front door
to see if anyone was at home. No one was, and Collie gently blocked
her path until she gave up, then accompanied her home for a friendly
visit.

When we passed the University of Florida, we made a quick swing
through the campus, and I remarked that I'd like to come back there
some day. I meant as a student, but I soon forgot about that, never
dreaming I'd return as an assistant professor of history in 1947 and
remain there for sixteen years.

One of the Rollins faculty members had sent her son to Peekskill
Military Academy, which made it financially possible for members
of the teaching profession. My mother wrote to the principal, and
after we got settled in Poughkeepsie, I went to Peekskill to enter

PMA. I was a senior by this time, but the school had a five-year high school program, so that meant two more years.

The regime at a military school was a new and totally unfamiliar way of life for me, but once I learned the routine I almost enjoyed it. One thing I learned was to be able to shave, shower, and change uniforms by the time the bugler blew "assembly." The only course I recall enjoying was ancient history.

The spring of 1933 was PMA's hundredth anniversary, and Lowell Thomas was speaker at the celebration. Because of a shortage of funds I went to Poughkeepsie High School in the fall of 1933, then returned to PMA in the spring and graduated. Harris, who went there the following year, was as penniless as I had been. Once, he told me, he didn't even have a three-cent stamp and in desperation tried to send a letter home C.O.D. He was much embarrassed to have it returned to him.

Arizona Again

In the fall of 1934, after I graduated from PMA, I worked for a few months as an usher in one of the Poughkeepsie theaters to earn enough money to get me to Arizona. Then I joined two young men who were driving there in an old Dodge touring car, and Collie accompanied us. The car had isinglass side curtains, but it was miserably cold the whole way, especially crossing the desert at night. After we got to Arizona I worked from time to time on a ranch near Tempe, where my uncle Harvey was foreman. When I left to take some classes at the university in Tucson, I left Collie with him. If I'd tried to take Collie with me I probably would have started a family row.

The ranch had cattle and a big feedlot, Quarter Horses, and alfalfa and maize fields, so a lot of the work wasn't on horseback. There was a huge open pit silo that we filled with chopped maize to make ensilage for fattening steers. Fortunately for me, there were some two- or three-year-old unbroken range horses of the typical cowpony type. They weren't valuable, compared to the Quarter Horses and Thoroughbreds, and I managed to take over lead-breaking them.

The bossman and the cowboys, mainly Mexican *vaqueros,* knew that I had come recently from New York, and they were surprised I knew anything about range horses. The bossman had a way of watching without appearing to, and after he saw me climb on one of the unbroken horses bareback without it showing any sign of wanting to buck, he looked up from whatever he was doing. "If you're going to ride them," he said, "you'd better use a hackamore and saddle." If I'd owned the ranch and had no poor kinfolk I couldn't have been happier.

The next morning I started working with the three unbroken horses. They weren't wild or mean; they simply hadn't been handled much. They learned quickly, and in two weeks I helped move cattle on one of them and even roped a young steer. The ranch had some really fine Quarter Horses and Thoroughbreds, which were used for rodeo roping, and I figured that if I stayed there long enough I could work up to being allowed to handle them. At a dollar and a half a day for ten hours of work, however, there wasn't much future in that, so I headed back to Tucson in the fall and took a few more classes, but not before I had the three horses handling like cowponies should.

There are times when a few words of advice can save your life, even many years later. When I was working with the range horses, one of them got scared at something and reared. Uncle Harvey, who happened to be watching, told me: "If one ever starts to go over backwards with you, push on the saddle with both hands. That way the saddlehorn won't go right through you." I remembered that advice long after I'd left Arizona and had gotten fairly civilized.

It came to mind at a most opportune moment in the 1950s, when we were living in Gainesville, Florida. Daughters Betty and Barbara both rode at every opportunity and enjoyed riding in horse shows. Betty rode in Western Pleasure classes, and Barby liked to show Saddlebreds and Tennessee Walkers, two breeds unfamiliar to me. A friend who knew both breeds well taught Barby a great deal about showing Saddlebreds.

One day he told me he'd had an opportunity to buy a registered young Saddlebred gelding for Barby at a price that seemed reasonable. He said the woman who owned the horse was riding him with a tie-down, which prevented him from throwing his head up. Queried about it, she claimed that she'd always ridden with a tie-down. As we soon learned, this wasn't exactly the whole story. At any rate, I reimbursed him and hoped the horse would do well in shows.

It wasn't long before Barby learned that he was a quitter. Whenever he became a little bit tired he'd start rearing, which was why the woman had used the tie-down. I worried about Barby getting hurt, and decided to give him a hard workout. I remembered what the *vaqueros* had said — sweaty saddle blankets can cure a lot of bad habits in any horse.

I put a tie-down on him so he couldn't rear and climbed on, intending to let him know what being really tired felt like. That didn't happen, however. When he began to tire a little and found he couldn't rear, he threw himself over backwards. All of a sudden I was looking straight at the sun. I shoved against the saddle with both hands just before we hit the ground. When I landed hard on my back the saddlehorn came down between my legs instead of going through my chest. The horse's head came down hard on me.

The fall broke six ribs, and it was weeks before I could get in and out of a car without painful spasms. One thing I knew for sure — my uncle's advice had saved my life. I sent the horse off to a sale in Georgia, and if he ended up in a case of Alpo dogfood I wouldn't have mourned him.

Bull Riding

Once when the bossman had some visitors they got to talking about bull riding. "You want to see how it's done?" he asked. They did.

"Come on," he said to me. He saddled one of his roping horses, and we all went down to the steer pens. By then I'd figured out who was expendable. I'd never tried bull riding, but had seen enough of it in the local rodeos to know that it wasn't easy. Fortunately, these were steers, not bulls, and they weren't likely to be mean.

He roped one by the horns, and my uncle put a rope around its middle for a surcingle. I grabbed it tightly with both hands and hopped on, while they pulled the lariat off the steer's horns. We were in the pen with a couple of hundred other steers, so the prospect of being thrown was unattractive. I stayed on it until it slipped and fell.

"Couldn't tell which was best, man or steer," the bossman said as he shook out a loop and roped another one. I stayed with it until it quit bucking and tried to leave through a barbed wire gate that didn't happen to be open. I came out of it with a few bruises and a scratch or two.

We did this a few more times when he had visitors. Those steers weren't really bad buckers, and I didn't get thrown. Bull riding didn't seem as bad as I'd thought, and I figured I was getting to be fairly good at it.

In the summer of 1936 when I was on an archaeological dig near Fort Apache, there was a big Fourth of July rodeo. While the Apaches were great on steer and calf roping, they were too smart to be interested in bull riding. But the spectators wanted to see some bull riding, and the agency director offered $2.50 to anyone who would come out of the chute on a bull. On the ranch at Tempe we worked ten hours for just $1.50, so $2.50 for a few seconds seemed like pretty fair pay.

One Apache and two Anglo cowboys who worked on the reservation and I accepted the offer. The three cowboys rode their bulls with ease and grace, which was no fun for the Apache spectators. When I climbed down into the chute my bull was quivering and making low moaning sounds, and I knew I was in for trouble. When I told them to turn him out he was on his way before the gate was open, scraping a chunk of skin off one of my legs.

It was a short but exciting ride. I sailed up in the air and came down skidding along on one eyebrow, which was ground down to the bone. Fortunately my hat hit first, and that may have helped, but it tore up the hatband. My legs came floating down after me, and I made a rather grotesque heap, right in front of the grandstand. I tried to get up with dignity and nonchalance, but didn't do very well at that, either.

People who don't know Indians have the mistaken belief that they are stoical and without a sense of humor. This is wrong. The Apaches joke all the time, and when they see something uproariously funny they laugh uproariously. That I learned as I dusted off my hat and walked the few steps back to the chutes. Every Apache in the place was holding his or her sides and laughing uncontrollably. I figured that I'd made the bull riding event worthwhile after all. "Now you see why Apaches don't like to ride bulls," my Apache friend David Kane said.

Apache Land

In the summer of 1936 my mother, sister, and I all enrolled in a summer archaeological field program at the University of Arizona. My mother was still at Vassar College, but joined us for the summer. Lavon was a full-time student at the University of Arizona, and I'd taken a few classes. The field work was on a Pueblo ruin called Kinishba, which was near Fort Apache and the town of Whiteriver. We were told that Coronado had described the ruins when he marched through that region on his way to the Zuni pueblo of Hawikuh in 1540.

To me the most attractive aspect of the field season was that we had twenty or thirty Apaches working along with us. When I was in high school I'd read every book about them I could find, so I already knew some of their history. I got along well with them, especially with David Kane. He always had an extra horse for me to ride. I'd picked up a Mexican stock saddle and roller bit, and we got some leather and made me a bridle. For fifteen dollars I bought a pair of high-heeled Justin boots at the trading post in Whiteriver. The boots were size nine, the largest pair in the place. I managed to get them on, but it was always a bit of a struggle. I still have them and can still get them on, but they must have shrunk some, for I have to lie down and rest afterward.

David and I rode all over, checking on his cattle and horses and visiting his friends. He had a two-year-old black stallion he wanted to give me. I had plans of breaking him and riding him back to the ranch in Tempe, but that didn't happen. We tried a number of times to corral him, but he was too elusive for us.

Don and Apache friend, David Kane, 1936

Some Saturday afternoons my mother and sister and I drove up to Pinetop, off the reservation, and ate steak at a bar and grill run by a character named Jake Renfro. One afternoon a man who worked on the roads and stayed in one of the camps on the reservation asked us for a ride. On the way he offered to show us a strange and wonderful place where Indians had lived long ago. Although it was late afternoon and would soon be dark, we agreed.

It was a long drive, down past Fort Apache and up what looked like the side of a mountain to Circle Prairie. By the time we got there the sun was setting. We were all by now a bit suspicious, but we went along with the man, walking over a rocky place toward the edge of a canyon. Suspecting that he was going to try to reduce the population by three I dropped behind and picked up a jagged piece of rock, determined to bash him with it if he tried to do us in.

We reached the edge of the canyon, where he pointed to a narrow ledge that led out to a sort of peninsula. We could hear water running far below in the darkness, and knew the canyon was deep. There was still just enough light above for us to see the remains of stone walls where an easily defended pueblo had been long ago. About thirty-five years later I used this pueblo and the summer program in a short story called "The Search."

On the long drive back to the road camp we were a bit more relaxed. My mother talked about having to head east soon for the fall term at Vassar. The last thing our road man said was, "Lady, when you go east I wish you'd say hello to my folks for me."

Kinishba

We rebuilt much of the old pueblo of Kinishba. The walls were of sandstone blocks with clay for mortar. It was flat-roofed, and part of it was two stories. Piñon rafters were laid in place across the walls, then smaller juniper poles were laid across them. These were crossed by a thick layer of willows, and topped by reeds. Then the whole roof was covered with a thick layer of clay. When thoroughly baked in the sun it was supposed to be waterproof, but some of the ones we built gave way in thunderstorms.

The students lived in tents. Dr. Byron Cummings, one of the pioneer archaeologists of the American Southwest, was in charge. His assistant was a doctoral student, Gordon Baldwin, later a freelance writer. We met again about twenty-five years later at a convention of Western Writers of America.

Paul Gebhard and I shared a tent for a time, then moved into one of the reconstructed rooms. One of the Apaches who had worked on the dig in previous years warned us that there were *chindees*—ghosts—in the room. That meant that the excavators had found a skeleton under the floor. That's where children were buried, so they could be close to their mothers. Paul became ill and didn't respond to such treatment as was available, and had to head for home. I haven't

Don and archaeologist Dean Byron Cummings
on later visit to Kinishba, 1941

seen him since then, but have seen his name connected to the Kin-
sey studies on sexuality in America.

The rooms were square, with one small opening, a slit about three
feet off the ground and about two and a half feet wide. That was
the door, and one had to step high and bend low to enter the room.
The rooms were amazingly well suited to the climate. The place was
about one mile in elevation, so the nights were rather cold. During
the night the room cooled off, so that when one came in for an after-
lunch siesta, it was still pleasantly cool, although it was quite hot
outside. By night the interior was warm, so that it was comfortable
on top of one's sleeping bag until early in the morning.

There was only one slight flaw to the rooms as sleeping quarters.
At night you could hear snakes chasing mice around in the rafters.

Since I slept most of the night on top of my sleeping bag I was a bit apprehensive about some snake making a wrong slither and falling on me. I had no flashlight, but I knew where the door was. I'm sure that if a snake had landed on me that room would have been known as the one with the wide door, for I would have vacated the premises in record time.

Although much of the time I drove the dump truck, I excavated one of the rooms, and found it like a treasure hunt, for there was no telling what might appear next. We were amazed at the variety of trade items that were unearthed in some of the rooms. My sister found a jade lip plug like the Aztecs wore. Someone else dug up a little copper bell. In the room I excavated there was a shell bead necklace of between eight hundred and nine hundred beads, each with a perfectly drilled hole in it.

One of the things that intrigued me most about Kinishba was learning that in his journal Coronado had mentioned seeing the ruins of the pueblo on the very spot in 1540. Whatever had caused the people to move, or whatever had destroyed them, had obviously happened long before Coronado's day. I tried to imagine how it must have been when his small army, accompanied by a horde of Indian bearers as well as a walking commissary of cattle, swine, and goats passed through that country. I decided I wanted to know more about Spanish explorations in Arizona and elsewhere, but it was several years before I had the opportunity.

We had a visitor at Kinishba for several days, and I had a chance to talk to him. He was Grenville Goodwin, a young ethnologist who had lived for a few years at the San Carlos Apache Reservation. To the amazement of my Apache friends he was fluent in their language. He told me much about his work in ethnology, to me an unfamiliar field that I found even more tempting than archaeology, and I planned to contact him later. Unfortunately, he died of a brain tumor a few years afterward. When the summer was over, I went back to cowboy life, for I wasn't quite ready to give it up and become a serious student.

That summer at Kinishba, as it turned out, was time well spent. I got to know a number of Apaches and learned more about them and their way of life. Also important, although I had no idea where it might lead, I developed a latent interest in Coronado and other early Spaniards in the Western hemisphere.

Last Visit

In the late summer of 1936 Harris and I cooked up another scheme for wandering. We decided to drive down across the border to Sonora, buy a couple of cowponies, and ride around from ranch to ranch and adventure to adventure. We had saddles and everything else we needed, and figured we'd saved enough money to buy a couple of ponies in Mexico. We headed for the border, but stopped in Tucson to talk to the Mexican consul.

"You will have to pay a deposit of one dollar per pound on your saddles when you cross the border," he told us.

As with many of our plans, it took only one little unexpected snag to blow it to bits. We had barely enough money to pay the deposit, but that would have left us with nothing for buying cowponies. If we'd left our saddles in Tucson and bought others in Mexico, the result would have been the same.

Since we were already in the mood for travel, we decided to visit the old homestead and consider the prospects of moving there and raising cattle or horses. We headed across the desert for Wickenburg and Kingman, crossing the Colorado at Needles. Then we drove on to Barstow and Victorville, up over Cajón Pass, and on to the road through the foothills. We found A. P. getting ready to drive to the store at Pearblossom, so we went with him. While we were there some men drove up; one of them was the man who'd asked me to pen the hammerhead kicker for him quite a few years before. I was about six feet tall or a little more by then, and he didn't recognize me.

A. P., who was still a tease, introduced us to the man, giving us made-up names. We shook hands and chatted a bit. And then A. P. gleefully told him, "These are the Worcester boys."

"They are? Well, by grab," he said, "I sure didn't recognize you."

We visited George Pallett, who now owned Rex. Curly Morrow was gone, nobody knew where. George let me ride Rex and loaned Harris another of his horses, so we had a chance to revisit some of the places we remembered. Rex was well cared for and in great shape, and it was a thrill to ride him again. I convinced myself that he remembered me, because that was what I wanted to believe. We renewed a lot of memories, and both Harris and I realized that we still had an attachment to the old homestead. We talked about settling there, buying Rex, and doing some ranching, but it was just happy talk, for we had no money to buy anything. Harris would return to the homestead once more and live there briefly, in an attempt to regain his health. I have never returned.

Before we headed back to Tempe, we drove to Los Angeles to have a last visit with our grandfather, who was living in an old folks' home. Our grandfather still talked about getting a well drilled on the homestead so he'd have water for irrigation. We told him we were thinking of raising horses there. That's when he remarked that all we'd ever been good at was "handling hosses."

We drove back to Arizona and I went to work on the Palo Verde ranch in the southern part of the state. After I got out of the navy at the end of World War II, I learned that George Pallett and Rex had both died. A. P. had moved away during the war, and no one knew where he was living. The homestead was sold while I was away.

Bard College

When I quit cowboy life in the late fall of 1936 and headed for Poughkeepsie, it was to enter Bard College for the spring semester. I had always been a lackadaisical student, but had finally matured enough to change. At the time I arrived, just after Christmas, Bard was closed for the between-semesters reading period, but Vassar College was soon in session. It was then that I met Barbara Livingston Peck, a most attractive and intelligent red-headed astronomy major, and was hooked.

It was high time that I became a serious student, for I was twenty-two before the spring semester was over, and only finishing the sophomore year. I had to carry twenty hours for a time, to make up for part-time work earlier. But I never considered the time I'd worked on ranches as wasted; it should give me something to write about one day, and I intended to own horses again.

Bard College, located near Annandale-on-Hudson, was on the old John Bard estate, and had formerly been St. Stephens, an Episcopalian college. Bard was an experimental project of Nicholas Murray Butler, so for a number of years it was attached to Columbia University. The whole student body numbered about 125; about 30 were sophomores.

Most classes were tutorials, with one or several students in them. Every two weeks each student had an hour-long conference with each instructor, whose first question was usually, "What have you been reading since last time?" Fresh off the Arizona range as I was, I was flabbergasted at first by those conferences, but I managed to adjust and soon. It was absolutely the best preparation for graduate school I could have had, and since I planned to do graduate work, I studied French and German as well as Spanish.

At Arizona I'd planned to major in archaeology, but Bard was so small that it didn't even have a course in anthropology. What my mother had told me about her days as a reporter made me think that would suit me. I figured that American literature would be a good background for a reporter, so I made it my major. My only experience as a journalist was as sports editor of the *Bardian* in my senior year, but the American literature came in handy twenty years later when, as a visiting professor in American studies at the University of Madrid, I taught American literature as one of the courses.

Because of the tutorials and bi-weekly conferences, we got well acquainted with our instructors. One day in the first semester of my junior year, the literature instructor asked me, "Do you know what you're really most interested in?"

That took me by surprise. Naturally, I didn't.

"History," he said. "It shows in what you like to talk about."

I didn't have to ponder that for long to know he was right. I switched to history as a major, with Latin America my area of interest. I'd heard of Dr. Herbert E. Bolton of the University of Cali-

Don

fornia, Berkeley; he had developed the field of the Spanish border-lands, and many of his graduate students worked in Latin American history. My mother had known him when she was at Berkeley. I decided I wanted to do graduate work under him.

Bard's president, an eastern type who was sure that all westerners were intellectually handicapped, asked me one day what I planned to do after graduation. When I told him I planned to go to graduate school, he looked at me condescendingly.

"Mr. Worcester," he said crisply, "not all of us are equipped to do graduate work. You should try to get on at a good preparatory school."

I thanked him for saving me from making a colossal blunder, but didn't mean it. That was a staggering blow—he could tell just by looking at me that I was incompetent to do graduate work! My record before coming to Bard was mediocre, but that wasn't true of my work there. I brooded about it a while, then told historian Abbott E. Smith. He smiled.

"Pay no attention to that," he told me. "You go on to Berkeley and don't worry about what he said. You'll do all right. I have no doubt about that."

His confidence in me was reassuring, but the doubts that the president had aroused accompanied me all the way to Berkeley.

We had a reading period of about a month between semesters. Students from wealthy families usually traveled. I worked as the student assistant to librarian Felix Hirsch, who had left Nazi Germany a few years earlier, and I was employed during summers and vacations as well as the regular term. I got started in Latin American history by spending my junior year reading period writing a report on the Mexican Revolution of 1910, particularly the nefarious role of U.S. Ambassador Henry Lane Wilson.

During the spring of my junior year, historians Abbott Smith and Carleton Qualey recommended that I go to summer school at the University of California and get acquainted with Dr. Bolton, who was close to retirement. I took their advice, and luckily for me, Dr. Bolton was teaching an undergraduate course on the Spanish Southwest that summer. I took it, got to know Dr. Bolton, and earned an A-plus for one of the few times I got fired up.

Dr. Bolton was writing his book on Coronado at the time, and although he later covered the whole trail, he hadn't yet followed it across Arizona to the Zuni pueblos. When he learned that I had spent a summer on an archaeological dig near Fort Apache, he asked me about some of the landmarks in that area that Coronado had mentioned in 1540.

"Coronado talked about a pueblo ruin; it should be near Fort Apache," he told me. "A few days later he came to a *barranca* [deep gorge] and had to ride a long way to get around it."

I told him the pueblo was Kinishba, where I'd spent a summer excavating. The highway from Whiteriver to Pinetop and Springerville crossed the *barranca*. I got to talk to him quite a bit after that.

In the summer course with Dr. Bolton I wrote a paper on Fray Marcos de Niza. When Cabeza de Vaca, two other Spaniards, and the Moorish slave Estevan finally reached Mexico in 1535 — they and the other Narváez expedition refugees had been stranded on the Texas coast in 1528 — they had many tales to tell. One concerned what they'd heard about the Seven Cities of Cíbola, actually the Zuni pueblos. The myth of the seven cities dated back to the eighth-century Moslem invasions of the Iberian Peninsula. According to the legend, seven Portuguese bishops and their congregations had sailed westward and founded seven fabulously rich cities. The Spaniards had brought the legend with them, and Cabeza de Vaca'a report immediately attracted the viceroy's attention. But before sending a costly expedition, he wanted the story verified.

Cabeza de Vaca and the other Spaniards declined to lead a small party north, but Estevan was a slave and had no choice. He was ordered to guide Fray Marcos de Niza and a party of Indians to the seven cities. In their wanderings earlier, Estevan and Cabeza de Vaca had learned the techniques of medicine men. Whenever Fray Marcos' party camped the Moor — being black — attracted a large crowd and was given his choice of young women, while few were interested in the religious services Fray Marcos offered. As a result, he sent Estevan ahead with a few Indians and orders to send a runner bearing a wooden cross when he had news. The size of the cross would indicate the importance of the news. After some days Estevan sent an Indian to Fray Marcos with a cross the size of a man.

Fray Marcos ordered Estevan to wait, but he continued to the Zuni pueblo of Hawikuh. When he requested young women, as usual, the Zunis, who were narrow-minded about such things, killed him. The Indians with him fled to rejoin Fray Marcos, who hastily returned to Mexico City. Whether or not Fray Marcos saw Hawikuh from a distance can't be determined, but rumors spread that the real seven cities had been found, and the viceroy sent the Coronado expedition to conquer them. Writing this paper gave me a taste of and liking for research in Spanish accounts. A revised version of this paper was later published as "Flight from Florida," in *New and Experimental Literature* (1975).

My senior project at Bard was on "Sea Power and Chilean Independence." Many years later, after further research and considerable revision, it was published in the University of Florida Monograph

Series. Eventually it was translated into Spanish and published in Chile for use at the naval academy.

Attachment to Horses

My attachment to horses goes back almost to infancy and has been lifelong. I was away from them only during college, the war, graduate school, and a few years more. While in Gainesville we eventually acquired three Quarter Horse mares and raised a few colts. What I enjoyed most before I became fragile as well as more cautious, was breaking and training cowponies.

In 1963, when I accepted the chairmanship of the Texas Christian University history department in order to initiate a doctoral program, Barbara and I made a preliminary trip to Fort Worth to buy a house. "First get a place for the horses," Barby and Betty instructed us, "and then get a house." We followed instructions and bought eighty-five acres in Parker County, about twenty-five miles southwest of TCU, then acquired a house in Fort Worth. When we moved we had the horses hauled from Florida.

A few years later the rancher-father of one of our students retired and gave me his twelve-year-old Arabian stallion, El Tordillo, "The Little Gray One." He had been on range with a herd of mares for ten years, and was most independent. We borrowed a horse trailer and drove out to Fort Stockton to get him, and he had one mare bred the afternoon we returned. He had been with us twenty years when he died at age thirty-two.

I had long admired Arabians and had broken a half-Arabian on the ranch near Tempe, but had never owned one. Over the years we acquired three Arabian mares, sold off every other animal, and raised only purebreds thereafter. One of the mares—Rudi—was gray but her sire was black, so I knew she had black genes. I hauled her to San Antonio to be bred to Cass Ole, a future national champion and star of the Black Stallion movies based on Walter Farley's popular series of books. She produced another handsome black stallion,

Al Zirr. Long before that time we'd built a house, acquired sixty more acres, and were living on the ranchito. (In Texas it would be presumptuous to call 145 acres a ranch.)

Since Barbara is an astronomer and many star names are Arabic, she provided us with names for many of the colts. Al Zirr, "The Button," is a star name. One bay filly with four white stockings was named Bhadra Pada after a star in the constellation Pegasus; it means beautiful or happy feet. We raised a bay stallion who was appropriately named Rahud—not a star name—meaning lightning.

We still have Al Zirr and half a dozen other purebreds, but arthritis and other consequences of antiquity have induced me to cut back activity. To me the most engaging sight every spring is new foals cautiously exploring their surroundings. They start testing their legs by running tight circles around their mommas. Each day the circles grow a little larger, until finally the little ones scamper off, tails up, while the mares whinny and trot after them.

Barby, Betty, and son Harris all inherited or became infected with my love of horses. All three own Arabians and probably will as long as circumstances permit. An attachment to horses is something one isn't likely to outgrow. At least I never did.

Graduate School

After graduating in 1939, I headed for Berkeley and graduate school with no little trepidation. I was not long off the range and had been a serious student for only a few years, so I still had a lot to make up. Remembering the Bard president's admonition, I was sure that all the other graduate students would be brilliant if not geniuses, and I would bring up the rear. Maybe the president was right after all. It turned out better than I had expected, but I realized how fortunate I had been in having had the two and a half years at Bard.

That first semester I was lucky enough to get a job as a student assistant in the Bancroft Library for twenty dollars a month. The library was a rich collection of books and manuscripts on the West,

Southwest, and Latin America, so it was where I did most of my research. Since my cousin Alan was also a student, earning by various jobs about the same as I, we rented a one-room apartment together in an ancient building on the corner of Dwight Way and Telegraph Avenue for twenty dollars a month. That left us the same amount for food — we did our own laundry. We ate mostly beans and potatoes and a lot of those big, oily sardines in oval cans, which were dirt cheap. I've never been able to look a sardine in the eye since then. Fatty hamburger was about ten cents a pound: once a week we splurged. Barbara was working on a master's degree in astronomy; she and her mother had an apartment, and they frequently gave us a real feast. Barbara's mother liked to see people enjoy their food, and we did our best to please her. Those delightful meals made us forget what we had to eat the rest of the week.

Dr. Bolton was in his last year before retiring, and I was told that his seminar was closed except to those who had studied with him before. Fortunately I'd taken his summer course the previous year, and when I went to his office, he remembered me. "You're one of my old students," he said, and that was good news.

There were between twenty-five and thirty students in his seminar that year, too many to fit around the famous "round table" he'd had built for his seminars. Actually it was more crescent-shaped than round, with us on the outside and him in the center. Members of that seminar were working on Western hemisphere areas ranging from the Klondike to Tierra del Fuego.

Once I told him I was looking for a topic for a master's thesis. "You're acquainted with the Apaches and their country," he said. "Not much has been written about them, especially in the early period. Why don't you write on them? There are lots of documents in Bancroft Library. In Spanish, of course."

I'd never lost my interest in the Apaches, and getting to know some of them that summer at Kinishba had strengthened it. I was elated at the prospect, and in the spring of 1940 turned in a thesis on the Apaches in the seventeenth century. I got two publications out of it, the first a lead article in the *New Mexico Historical Review,* and I was hooked on writing. Some of the graduate students were a bit cool toward me after that.

Dr. Maud W. Makemson at telescope

That first year my mother was on leave, working on her Polynesian navigation book. She spent some time at the Bishop Museum in Hawaii and her research was later published as *The Morning Star Rises*. I was taking a course on the Incas, Aztecs, and Mayas under Ronald Olson, and we often had coffee and chatted after class. When I told him what she was doing, he said, "Tell her she ought to work on the Maya calendar. It contains a lot of astronomical symbols, but no one has ever correlated it with ours."

I wrote to her about it, and that was her next project. She was on a Guggenheim Fellowship doing research in Mexico when the attack on Pearl Harbor came, and she headed right home. After publishing her findings, she translated a Maya chronicle that was published as *The Book of the Jaguar Priest*.

The second year I had a teaching assistantship and continued working for Bancroft Library, so I was financially solvent. Two other students and I lived with the Lowies. Dr. Robert Lowie had come from Vienna when young and had some kind of job on the Columbia University campus. He became acquainted with pioneer anthropologist Franz Boas, who got him interested in anthropology, and in due course Lowie earned a doctorate in the subject. He had done considerable work among the Crow Indians afterward, and had become fluent in their language. Once he tracked down an old Crow informant on a remote part of the reservation. When he walked up to the cabin the old Indian came out, while his dog barked furiously at Dr. Lowie. "Why are you barking at me, little dog?" Lowie asked in Crow.

The old Indian was so surprised to hear a paleface speaking his language that he turned to the dog. "He asks why you are barking at him," he told it. When I returned to graduate school after the war, Dr. Lowie was one of the two anthropologists on my doctoral committee.

Those first two years in graduate school were under the cloud cast by the war in Europe. In the fall of 1939 Professor Charles E. Chapman used the blackboard to indicate to the class what the cost of the war would be to America if we entered it immediately, and how much greater it would be the longer we waited. The class hissed him, but I believed that his apppraisal was correct, as it proved to be. All indications were that we would be involved before it was over. I was torn between trying to complete degree work and entering one of the military services without waiting to be drafted.

In the spring of 1941 I applied for a probationary (or some term like that) commission in the naval reserve. I was too weak in mathematics to qualify for line (deck duty), so I entered the supply corps. Barbara and I were married on July 5, 1941, and about a month later I received orders to report to Boston in September for training.

While my mother was away studying Mayan astronomy, Barbara took her place at Vassar, having recently completed her master's degree. Some weekends I took the train to New Haven, where she met me with the car to drive to Poughkeepsie. One Sunday we drove down to New Haven so I could take the train back to Boston. We were talking and didn't have the radio turned on. When we got to the

Barbara Livingston Peck and Don

station I saw an ensign I knew, and remarked that he was a bit early.

"I thought I should be early after what happened," he said. Just as I was asking what had happened I saw a newspaper in a rack across the waiting room. The headline was large enough to read at that distance: "Japs Bomb Pearl Harbor." I was speechless. Barbara and I said a hasty farewell and she drove alone back to Vassar. Although there'd been every indication that we'd soon be in the war, when it came with the smashing of our Pacific fleet it was an enormous shock. Unprepared as the nation was, it looked as though the war would drag on for years.

Harris

In the spring of 1941 Harris and I were both in Berkeley. He was an undergraduate and I was in my second year of doctoral work. One day Harris turned in to the infirmary. I stopped by to see him every afternoon for several days. I was there once when the doctor came in. He waited outside the room until I came out.

"We're making tests," he said. "Your brother has either tuberculosis or Hodgkins Disease, which is fatal and incurable. We'll have the results Friday."

I slept little for the next few nights. On Friday afternoon I went to the infirmary again. Harris seemed cheerful, but said nothing of the test results, so I supposed that he hadn't been informed. As I was leaving, he said, "By the way, the doctor came by a little while before you arrived. He says I don't have TB. Isn't that great!"

I don't know what I said, if anything, but I stumbled blindly back to my room, hoping I wouldn't have to talk to anyone until I could find my voice. The doctor's words "fatal and incurable" rang in my ears. In a few days I found out more about the disease. Its victims seem to improve for a time, and hopes always rise. Then they sink again, each time a bit lower than before, as it gets progressively worse.

In mid-August Barbara and I, newly married, drove east for me to report to the Navy Supply Corps School and for Barbara to start work at Vassar. Harris, who had been informed that his outlook was bleak, decided to go back to the homestead and stay as long as he was able to look after himself, with A. P.'s help. It was, he said, the only place he cared to be, under the circumstances. He had to get the sheriff to evict a squatter who claimed that his brother, the Lord, had given him the place. The squatter didn't have a deed to it, but he did have a shotgun, and he looked like one who would be willing to use it on humans. When the sheriff arrived, however, he left peacefully. Things happened quickly after the Japanese attack on Pearl Harbor, or so it seemed. It looked to me as if the war would go on for ten years at least, for there were no rays of hope in any direction. In February I went to my first assignment, in San

Don and Harris

Juan, Puerto Rico. I learned soon after arriving that Harris was with our aunt Mable, who had moved from Phoenix to San Diego, for he had become progressively worse and couldn't manage alone on the homestead.

In the summer I was granted ten days of emergency leave for a last visit. I was supposed to be able to fly all the way to San Diego on a navy transport plane, but I was put off in Pensacola, and there was no hope of getting another flight. I got on a train, but at that hectic period of the war passenger trains sat on sidings waiting for freight trains to pass, and it took three days to reach San Diego.

Knowing that I would have to allow several days to get back to Pensacola, I immediately applied for an extension of leave. It was denied. I learned later that it was denied because I had applied immediately after arriving rather than later. The logic of that reaction still evades me.

Barbara and my mother came, and we spent four days together. We reminisced about old times, our favorite horses, escapades, and such, but it was all rather hollow, for all of us knew that his days were few. He told my aunt that if one of us had to go he was glad to be the one, for he thought I might amount to something as a writer.

Harris and I parted at the railroad station, when Barbara and I took the train for Pensacola. We didn't say much, just shook hands. I couldn't speak, but couldn't think of anything worth saying anyway.

It was a miserable trip for many reasons. Our train was late getting to New Orleans, so we missed our connection and had to take a bus that was so crowded that both of us had to stand for two hundred miles before seats were available. At the Pensacola Naval Air Station I got on a navy transport plane bound for San Juan, and made it back before my ten-day leave expired.

Harris died a few months later, about the time I was transferred to the U.S. Naval Station at Aruba, NWI, off the coast of Venezuela. It was some weeks before my mail caught up with me, so the news of his death reached me about six weeks late. It seemed one whole period of my life had been put away in a separate compartment marked: "Do not open." I could never look back on those years in the same way I had in the past.

Palmdale

In February 1988 the *New York Times* ran an article headlined: "Where City Meets Desert Somewhat Awkwardly." It was about the booming town of Palmdale, which since 1982 had tripled in population to 42,000 and is expected to double again by 1993. Before the boom began, Palmdale had been known only as the construction site of the space shuttle, the B-1-B bomber, and more recently the B-2 Stealth bomber. But the new residents aren't involved in the town's aero-

Harris

space industry—most commute sixty to eighty miles daily to jobs in Los Angeles.

Since I hadn't seen Palmdale for at least fifty years, reading the *Times* article revived a lot of faded memories. The Palmdale I had known in the 1920s was a quiet little railroad town on the edge of Antelope Valley and the Mojave Desert, with a block or two of stores, Kidd's butchershop, a garage, and a blacksmith but not much else. Palmdale was twenty miles from the old homestead, and we seldom went there unless someone was leaving or arriving by train, or my grandfather needed the blacksmith to repair or sharpen tools.

I was six or seven the year my mother taught school there, and that's where I saw my first silent movie. I forget what it was about, but I remember a man watching the screen and playing a piano, making sounds that presumably were in keeping with the action. The film broke occasionally and flapped around the wheel until the projectionist got it stopped. When it was repaired and action resumed, everybody clapped. We were easy to entertain in those days.

On reading the *Times* article, I was struck as a historian by the amazing difference between the Palmdale — and the nation — of only sixty years ago and today. Our way of life, especially our material culture, has changed enormously in that short period. It used to be a long, hard drive over narrow winding roads from Los Angeles to Palmdale. Now that burgeoning town is virtually a detached suburb of Los Angeles.

At that time World War I was the Great War, the war to end all wars. Folks in that hinterland were still using teams and wagons for travel. Everyman's car, the Model T Ford, was just making its appearance on the gravel and rutted wagon roads of the back country. When the state or county began paving the road east past Little Rock toward Victorville, huge road crews did the work with horse and mule teams, using fresnos to move dirt and scrapers for leveling it. They'd set up a tent camp, build a big corral for the many teams, complete a stretch of road, and then move on. We watched the work from the school bus, and although the pavement greatly improved the bus ride, we regretted seeing the crews move on.

Life was relatively simple — a daily struggle to put food on the table — and there was no need for advertisements to tell us what we wanted or couldn't live without. It was enough just to have a mail-order catalog, for they included everything from clothing and household goods to harness and farm tools. The Watkins man came by once or twice a year with sewing materials, vanilla extract, and such things for housewives. There was no wide range of items available for the entertainment of those who had a little extra money to spend. We didn't own a phonograph, but at one time a neighbor family did. The few records they had were tubular rather than flat; the only one I recall was "The Preacher and the Bear."

Then battery-operated radios came along, although we had little acquaintance with them. Some of the successful pear growers in Little Rock bought them, and the first one I ever heard was when Calvin Coolidge made his inaugural address, if I remember correctly. A man who lived across the road from the school set up a radio in his yard and all the urchins were herded over there to share in this historic moment. If it weren't for the fact that we got out of school for an hour, it would have been a tremendous bore.

About that time or a few years earlier, blacksmith shops were being converted to garages to repair automobiles. Some enterprising men obtained repair manuals and began repairing radios in their homes.

The astounding improvement in the material wealth of the average American family in the years immediately after World War II was driven home to me when I was a visiting professor at the University of Madrid in 1956–57. After most of our wars in the past, production stimulated by military needs declined drastically, but in this case the tremendous industrial growth necessary for the United States to become the "arsenal of democracy" was rapidly transformed to production for civilians and almost overnight made us an affluent society.

In Madrid a Spanish friend remarked that all American families were rich. I protested that university professors were by no means in that category.

"Do you own your house?" he asked. We did, or at least we and a mortgage company owned it. "Own a car?" I had to admit that we had two cars, although one of them wasn't up to much more than getting me to the campus and back each day. At that time a Spanish family was lucky to own a motor scooter, and we often saw a family of three or four clinging to one. All automobiles had to be imported, and import duties were outrageously high.

"You're rich," my friend said. In a way he was right, for average-income families like ours enjoyed comforts far beyond those of many countries or even what we could have afforded or obtained in the depression years before the war. And further back, during my childhood, we and a great many others were fortunate to have had the bare necessities.

Those days had long receded to the fringes of my memory, in part, perhaps, because I wanted to forget them. At any rate I wasn't often reminded of them. But the *Times* article forced me to recall that first trip to the old homestead, the thrill of going through the Newhall tunnel, and stopping at The Oaks to eat sandwiches while the 1914 Model T's radiator stopped boiling.

In looking back over a lifetime, I was astonished at the enormous changes that had occurred in that short span, hardly a paragraph in the history of mankind. It shouldn't have surprised me, perhaps, for as a historian I had become well aware that people living in times of transition from one epoch to another are unable to see that what is gradually happening to their way of life is irreversible, that the good old days are indeed gone. Uneasy about what was happening, most probably hoped that things would soon be as before. We read about the Fall of Rome and are surprised to learn that Romans apparently were unaware that Rome had fallen. It is much easier to comprehend the past than the present or future.

The *Times* article triggered one memory after another, and I thought again of the day I gave up life on ranches and the horses I loved, put all that behind me, at least for the moment, and headed east for college and the world of books.

Coyote

As cowponies go, Coyote wasn't much to look at. He was a dusty bay and a bit ewe-necked from his mustang or Indian pony ancestors, but he had heart and brains. He was one of the five mounts in my string on the Palo Verde ranch in southern Arizona, where I had my last fling at cowboy life in the fall of 1936. The ranch covered many miles of rough country; it took a lot of that desert land to support a cow and a calf, and there were only four of us to cover it—the Old Man, Jeff, who was foreman or straw boss, Cipriano, a *vaquero* from Sonora who was an artist with a lariat, and me. They were all top hands, and from them I learned a lot about roping and handling cattle in rough country.

Except when we were branding calves or separating steers for market, about all we did was ride from dawn to dusk looking for cattle that needed doctoring for screw worms, which could eat a cow alive if they had the chance. We carried red medicine and a few other remedies in our saddlebags, and when we saw an animal that needed doctoring we roped it and worked on it right there and then. The country was so brushy or rocky in places that we had to rope a cow and follow it to an open space before we could throw it. Our ponies were all trained to keep going when a loop was thrown and not stop until told to. Having so much country to cover, we always rode alone, so it meant rope, throw, and tie by yourself. All cowboys could do that in the old days but it's almost a lost art today.

Although I rode Coyote only one day in five, I soon realized that he knew the business a lot better than I did. He always kept an ear cocked back toward me, so I talked to him a lot, and found he'd do lots of things just from voice commands.

Once I rode Coyote clear off the Palo Verde range to see what lay beyond and came to country so rough that I figured it must have been set aside for an Indian reservation. At the edge of a mesa I looked down into a rocky canyon and saw half a dozen wild horses guarded by a battle-scarred little roan stallion. They were all off on the run, but the spookiest one had white marks on its back, as though it had been ridden and gotten saddle sores. Coyote was usually all business, but now he could hardly stand still; he seemed to want to follow the wild ones. When I turned him back toward the ranch he exhaled deeply and his head sagged. I was sorry for him, for I could guess how he felt.

"There've always been a few wild ponies out yonder," the Old Man told me. "In that country it would be impossible to corral them, so there'll always be a few there. The one with the saddle marks was some old cowpony. When a tame one gets into a wild bunch it's always the hardest to catch. Knows what freedom is, I guess. Once in a while some of the young stallions get in with our mares and we corral them. Come to think of it, that's how I got Coyote."

Once when I jumped off to wrestle down and doctor a calf I'd roped I twisted my ankle and it swelled up like a bloated heifer. My boots were already as tight as women's bathing suits in mail-order catalogs, so there was no way I could get one on over that ankle. I wore an old pair of Apache moccasins I'd acquired in Whiteriver.

The Old Man was worried when he saw them. "Watch out you don't get a foot caught in your stirrup, son," he warned me. "You wouldn't be the first man dragged to death that way."

Luckily for me I rode Coyote that day. I came onto a yearling bull that had a gash on his shoulder. He didn't run much but when I dropped a loop over his head and jerked up the slack he turned and charged, hitting me on the right leg and knocking me clean out of the saddle. As I went down my left foot slid through the stirrup and I was in big trouble, flat on my back with a foot caught.

Even before I hit the ground I was talking fast and sweet to Coyote, and he cocked an ear down my way, as if wondering what I was doing there. The young bull hit the end of the rope and came back, still on the prod. Coyote took a hard lick in the ribs that punctured his hide in two places. By then I'd caught hold of my saddle strings and was pulling myself up, still talking fast. If Coyote had spooked, my head would have gone bouncing over the rocks.

Once I was back in the saddle I left both feet out of the stirrups. We handled the young bull easily enough, but I felt pretty shaky. From that moment on I loved old Coyote as if he were my only kinfolk.

It didn't seem to be worth telling anyone about it, but I told the Old Man that when I left I wanted to buy Coyote. He watched me doctoring Coyote's wounds and the skinned place on my leg, and I guess he figured out what had happened. He smiled. "When you leave, son, he's yours," he said. I should have left right then, for a few weeks later the Old Man had an attack of some kind. By the time Jeff got him into town to see the doctor, it was too late.

I stayed on a while to help Jeff. He wrote to the Old Man's widow, somewhere in the Midwest, and one day a man showed up and announced that he was the son and heir. Jeff and I called him Old Man Junior, mostly Junior, but not to his face. He didn't know a cow from a burro, but that didn't keep him from telling us what to do. Finally he told me they could get along with one less man. I led Coyote out of the corral and threw my saddle on him.

"That horse has my brand on it," Junior said. I told him the Old Man had given Coyote to me.

"Where's your bill of sale?" He had me there. "I didn't get where I am by being sentimental about animals," he announced. "When that horse is no use to my ranch I'll sell him for chicken feed."

I didn't know where he'd gotten by being hard to live with, but I left without Coyote. Not having anything better to do, I worked around the university for a while and sat in on a few courses. I'd always told myself I wanted to be a writer and liked to think that by cowboying I was learning something I could write about some day. I got a lot of advice from my mother about that—come back here and finish college or you'll grow up to be a bowlegged idiot, and that sort of thing. I had to admit that what she said was true. Finally I decided it was time to go one way or the other.

I would make one more attempt to buy Coyote. I even considered stealing him, having a shoot-out with Junior, and other pleasant fantasies. If I could get Coyote I'd ride around from one ranch to another for maybe a year and then finish college. I might even cross over into Sonora and see that country, as Harris and I had planned to do earlier. If I couldn't get him I'd go on home, try to forget him, finish college, and see what came up after that.

I wrote to Jeff that I'd be coming in about a week. He replied that he'd be in town the following Saturday—they'd caught one of the young wild stallions and he'd see me there and maybe Coyote. Writing a letter was hard work for Jeff, and I guess he was too tired to stick in a few commas and periods, so I couldn't make a lot of sense out of what he wrote.

Everything I owned but saddle and chaps fitted into one battered suitcase. I rode the train there, left saddle and suitcase in the dusty waiting room at the station, then walked down to the loading pens to look for Jeff. The corrals seemed to be empty, but when I got closer I saw a roan bronco and a bay pony, standing with his head near the ground. Coyote!

Junior had done what he said he'd do, and I guess that's what Jeff was trying to tell me. Coyote and the little roan were waiting to be loaded into a cattle car and hauled to the slaughterhouse. I looked off to the west and could see the buttes and mesas where the wild ones roamed. My eyes were getting blurred from dust or something, but I opened the gate and walked into the pen.

Coyote came to me, whinnying softly, and we exchanged greetings sort of man to man, though I had trouble getting words out.

The wild pony, which reminded me of the old roan stallion I'd seen, stood as far from me as he could get, with the whites of his eyes showing and rollers in his nose. My eyes were getting runny from the dust so I turned and went out the gate. I must have forgotten to close it, for the two ponies dashed out and headed toward a little-used trail that led to the distant buttes. As they crossed a hill, Coyote stopped and looked back, as though he wondered if I was coming. For a moment, with neck arched and mane flying, he looked beautiful, like a wild stallion. I wanted to yell, "Run like a fool!" but my voice sounded as if I was trying to gargle turpentine. I waved my hat at him, and he was gone.

The crippled-up old cowboy who ran the saddle shop handed me a few bills for my saddle, though he may have wondered where he'd find a dude to buy it. At the station I bought a ticket home, then counted what I had left. It wasn't much, but I got a stamped envelope at the post office, printed Junior's name on it, and slipped in all but a little eating money for the trip home. He might wonder where it came from, but I knew he'd pocket those bills and consider himself real businesslike and unsentimental.

At the station I sat and waited for the next train to come snorting in. I was going where I knew I should go, and Coyote was heading for his old range. I'd always wanted to own that old pony. Now, in a way, I did.

A Visit from Father was composed into type on a Compugraphic digital phototypesetter in ten and one-half point Garamond with two and one-half points of spacing between the lines. Garamond was also selected for display. The book was designed by Jim Billingsley, composed by Metricomp, Inc., printed offset by Thomson-Shore, Inc., and bound by John H. Dekker & Sons, Inc. The paper on which this book is printed bears acid-free characteristics for an effective life of at least three hundred years.

TEXAS A&M UNIVERSITY PRESS : COLLEGE STATION